ONE RECIPE A HUNDRED SAUCES

ONE RECIPE
A HUNDRED
SAUCES

Linda Doeser

This edition published by Parragon Books Ltd in 2013
LOVE FOOD is an imprint of Parragon Books Ltd

Parragon Books Ltd
Chartist House
15–17 Trim Street
Bath BA1 1HA, UK
www.parragon.com/lovefood

ISBN 978-1-4723-3018-5

Printed in China

Written by Linda Doeser
Cover design by Geoff Borin
Photography by Mike Cooper
Home economy by Lincoln Jefferson

Notes for the Reader
This book uses both metric and imperial measurements. Follow the same units of measurement
throughout; do not mix metric and imperial. All spoon measurements are level: teaspoons are
assumed to be 5 ml, and tablespoons are assumed to be 15 ml. Unless otherwise stated, milk
is assumed to be full fat, eggs and individual vegetables are medium, and pepper is freshly
ground black pepper. Unless otherwise stated, all root vegetables should be washed in plain
water and peeled prior to using. For best results, use a food thermometer when cooking meat
and poultry – check the latest government guidelines for current advice.

Garnishes, decorations and serving suggestions are all optional and not necessarily included in the
recipe ingredients or method. The times given are an approximate guide only. Preparation times
differ according to the techniques used by different people and the cooking times may also vary
from those given. Optional ingredients, variations or serving suggestions have not been included in
the time calculations.

Recipes using raw or very lightly cooked eggs should be avoided by infants, the elderly, pregnant
women, convalescents and anyone suffering from an illness. Pregnant and breastfeeding women are
advised to avoid eating peanuts and peanut products. Sufferers from nut allergies should be aware
that some of the ready-made ingredients used in the recipes in this book may contain nuts. Always
check the packaging before use.

Contents

Introduction

A well-made, tasty sauce is often the secret that turns a good dish into a great one – and there are few sauces that are more versatile and more popular than tomato sauce. It makes a great accompaniment to plainly cooked meat, poultry, fish, vegetables and eggs, and works superbly well as the basis for braised dishes, stews and layered bakes. It's the perfect topping for pasta, essential for classic pizzas and makes a delicious hot or cold dipping sauce for all kinds of vegetables and fritters.

A simple tomato sauce is quick and easy to make. There's no risk of curdling and it doesn't require much attention while it simmers. It can be made in advance and reheated, the ingredients are inexpensive and readily available and it keeps well in the refrigerator and freezer. All the dishes in this book can be made with just the basic sauce – and will be truly delicious – but the recipes also include a huge number of variations. Tomatoes go so well with other ingredients – from chillies to mushrooms and from almonds to olives – that the options are almost endless. There are substantial versions that include bacon, cheese, sweetcorn, beans or other vegetables; spicy sauces with warm Middle Eastern flavours, hot Mexican chillies, subtle Indian mixes or a savoury barbecue tang; rich sauces with cream, butter, yogurt, wine or sherry; and piquant mixtures with olives, capers, oranges, horseradish, anchovies or apples.

Basic Tomato Sauce Ingredients

Tomatoes are, of course, the main and most important ingredient in a basic tomato sauce and there is debate about whether fresh or canned tomatoes make the best sauce. Fresh tomatoes that have ripened fully in the sun are sweet and full of flavour – particularly if they're home grown – and will almost certainly make a really tasty sauce. However, out-of-season tomatoes that have to be imported may have been picked before they are ripe and are often watery and tasteless. Good-quality canned tomatoes are available all year round and are excellent for making tomato sauce. In blind tastings, many people have either been unable to taste any difference between the same sauce made with fresh and canned tomatoes or have actually preferred the one made with canned.

Plum tomatoes, whether fresh or canned, are perfect for cooking as they have denser, less watery flesh than round tomatoes. Many round tomato varieties are selected by suppliers because they are robust enough to withstand the rigours of transportation rather than for their flavour, although recent years have seen an increase in the range of tomatoes available. Cherry tomatoes tend to be more expensive but are usually sweet and fragrant. Never use unripe tomatoes for making tomato sauce as no amount of added sugar will counteract their acidity and sharpness – keep them for making chutney. However, you can use varieties that turn yellow when ripe, but the sauce may be less visually appealing than when made with red tomatoes.

Tomato purée intensifies the flavour of tomatoes and is particularly useful if you are using fresh tomatoes that may not have been sun-ripened. Sugar helps to counteract the acidity of tomatoes, some of which can be very sharp. A useful tip when you don't have any tomato purée is to omit the sugar and add 1–2 tablespoons of tomato ketchup instead.

Various members of the onion family add flavour and emphasis to tomato sauce. The common brown onion is a good all-rounder and can be used in any recipe but some recipes work even better with other varieties. Sweet onions include red onions, which have reddish-purple skins and pink-tinged flesh, and Spanish onions, which are very large and mild with a mellow flavour. Shallots are much smaller than most varieties of onion and are elongated in shape. They are far less astringent than onions, although they do vary in strength and have a distinctive taste that is not quite onion and not quite garlic. Spring onions, with a white bulb and leafy green tops, are mild and cook quickly. Garlic is a natural partner for tomatoes and gives extra depth to the flavour of the sauce. The number of cloves to include is a matter of personal taste. If you are not very keen on the flavour, add a whole clove when softening the onion and then remove and discard it before adding the other ingredients. This will give just a hint of garlic that you won't find overwhelming.

Most recipes in this book recommend using olive oil, which not only has a rich flavour and aroma that complement tomatoes but is also a healthy choice as it contains monounsaturated fat. It just seems to go perfectly with the flavour of tomatoes and is the natural choice for Mediterranean and Middle Eastern recipes. You do not need to use expensive extra virgin oil – keep that for salad dressings. Virgin oil, from the second pressing, is perfect for cooking, but avoid olive oils simply labelled 'pure' as they have often been heat-treated and consequently have lost all flavour. If you're using other vegetable oils, perhaps because the sauce is very spicy, choose one with a bland flavour, such as sunflower, safflower, groundnut or corn oil.

As a rule, fresh herbs are always more flavoursome than dried, although both bay leaves and oregano are often used dried. Basil is the tomato herb as it complements the flavour superbly. The

leaves are easily bruised so it is often better to tear it by hand rather than to chop it with a knife. Both curly and flat-leaf parsley and fresh coriander are also good choices. One or two bay leaves add a distinctive flavour and aroma to robust tomato sauces but don't forget to remove them before serving.

The final ingredient in the basic tomato sauce is celery, which provides extra flavour and texture. If you dislike the 'strings' in celery, they can be removed easily by running a vegetable peeler along the length of the stick.

Preparing Fresh Tomatoes

To peel tomatoes, cut a cross in the top of the tomatoes and put them into a heatproof bowl. Pour in boiling water to cover and leave to stand for 1 minute. Drain and peel off the skins with a sharp knife; they should slip off easily. Don't try to peel more than 4–5 tomatoes at one time or some will begin to cook in the boiling water.

If you have a gas cooker, you can also peel tomatoes by skewering them, one at a time, with a metal fork, holding them in the gas flame and turning for 1–2 minutes, until the skin splits and wrinkles. Leave to cool, then pull off the skins with your fingers.

Always cut out the top part of the tomato where the stem grew and the central pale core, which is quite hard and inedible, using a sharp knife.

Most recipes in this book do not suggest deseeding tomatoes, but a few do. There are also recipes where the finished sauce should be pressed through a sieve. This removes the seeds as well as the vegetables and other solid matter.

To deseed tomatoes, cut them in half with a sharp knife, then scoop out the seeds using a teaspoon.

Basic Tomato Sauce

Makes about 600 ml/1 pint

* 25 g/1 oz butter
* 2 tbsp olive or other vegetable oil
* 1 onion, finely chopped
* 1 garlic clove, finely chopped
* 1 celery stick, finely chopped
* 400 g/14 oz canned chopped tomatoes or 500 g/ 1 lb 2 oz plum tomatoes, peeled, cored and chopped
* 2 tbsp tomato purée
* brown sugar, to taste
* 1 tbsp chopped fresh herbs and/or 1–2 tsp dried herbs and/or 1–2 bay leaves
* 100 ml/3½ fl oz water
* salt and pepper

Melt the butter with the oil in a saucepan. Add the onion, garlic and celery and cook over a low heat, stirring occasionally, for 5 minutes, until softened. Stir in the tomatoes, tomato purée, sugar to taste, the herbs and water and season to taste with salt and pepper. Increase the heat to medium and bring to the boil, then reduce the heat and simmer, stirring occasionally, for 15–20 minutes, until thickened.

This is the basic recipe that all 100 dishes in this book are based on. For each recipe the ingredients are highlighted (✳) for easy reference. Please note that quantities may vary so please check these carefully.

Easy

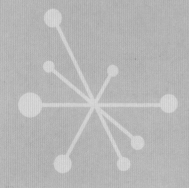

Barbecued Beef Kebabs

① First, make the sauce. Melt the butter with the oil in a saucepan. Add the Spanish onion, garlic and celery and cook over a low heat, stirring occasionally, for 5 minutes, until softened. Add the chillies and cook, stirring occasionally, for a further 3 minutes. Stir in the tomatoes, tomato purée, mustard powder, bay leaf, Worcestershire sauce, honey and vinegar and season to taste with salt and pepper. Increase the heat to medium and bring to the boil, then reduce the heat and simmer, stirring occasionally, for 15–20 minutes, until thickened.

② Remove the pan from the heat and leave to cool slightly. Remove and discard the bay leaf, then transfer the sauce to a food processor and process until smooth. Press the sauce through a sieve into a bowl.

③ Preheat the barbecue or grill. Brush four metal skewers with oil. Cut each red onion into eight wedges. Trim the spring onions and cut in half widthways. Thread the steak cubes onto the skewers, alternating them with onion wedges and spring onion halves.

④ Transfer about three quarters of the sauce to a sauceboat. Brush half the remainder over the kebabs and cook over hot coals or under the preheated grill, turning frequently and brushing with the remaining sauce from the bowl, for 8–10 minutes, until the meat is cooked to your liking. Serve immediately with the reserved sauce.

Serves 4

olive oil, for brushing
2 red onions
4 spring onions
700 g/1 lb 9 oz rump steak, cut into cubes

Barbecue sauce
* 25 g/1 oz butter
* 2 tbsp olive oil
1 Spanish onion, finely chopped
* 2 garlic cloves, finely chopped
* 1 celery stick, finely chopped
1–2 fresh red chillies, deseeded and chopped
* 400 g/14 oz canned chopped tomatoes
* 2 tbsp tomato purée
1 tsp mustard powder
* 1 bay leaf
2 tbsp Worcestershire sauce
3 tbsp clear honey
1 tbsp red wine vinegar
* salt and pepper

Minestrone

1 Cook the pancetta in a large heavy-based saucepan over a low heat, stirring occasionally, for 2–3 minutes, until the fat runs. Add the potatoes, carrot, celery and courgette and cook, stirring occasionally, for 10 minutes.

2 Pour the tomato sauce into the pan with the vegetables, then stir in the stock and add the cannellini beans, parsley, sage and basil. Increase the heat to medium and bring to the boil, then reduce the heat and simmer for 5 minutes.

3 Add the peas and pasta, bring back to the boil and simmer for a further 10 minutes. Taste and adjust the seasoning, adding salt and pepper if needed. Ladle into warmed bowls and serve immediately.

Serves 4

55 g/2 oz pancetta or unsmoked bacon, diced

2 potatoes, diced

1 carrot, sliced

1 celery stick, sliced

1 courgette, sliced

✳ 1 quantity Basic Tomato Sauce (see page 10)

850 ml/1½ pints chicken or vegetable stock

400 g/14 oz canned cannellini beans, drained and rinsed

1 tbsp chopped fresh flat-leaf parsley

1 fresh sage sprig, chopped

1 fresh basil sprig, chopped

115 g/4 oz frozen peas

55 g/2 oz dried anellini or other soup pasta

salt and pepper

White Beans with Prosciutto & Tomato Sauce

1. Put the beans into a large saucepan, pour in water to cover and bring to the boil over a medium–high heat. Reduce the heat and simmer for 45 minutes, until the beans are just tender. Drain well and set aside.

2. Melt the butter with the oil in a saucepan. Add the onions, garlic and celery and cook over a low heat, stirring occasionally, for 5 minutes, until softened. Stir in the tomatoes, tomato purée, sugar to taste, basil, prosciutto and water and season to taste with salt and pepper. Increase the heat to medium and bring to the boil.

3. Add the beans, reduce the heat and simmer, stirring occasionally, for 30 minutes. Transfer to a warmed serving dish and serve immediately.

Serves 4–6

500 g/1 lb 2 oz dried haricot beans, soaked overnight and drained
* 55 g/2 oz butter
* 4 tbsp olive oil
* 2 onions, finely chopped
* 2 garlic cloves, finely chopped
* 2 celery sticks, finely chopped
* 800 g/1 lb 12 oz canned chopped tomatoes
* 2 tbsp tomato purée
* brown sugar, to taste
* 1 tbsp chopped fresh basil
115 g/4 oz prosciutto, chopped
* 100 ml/3½ fl oz water
* salt and pepper

Italian-style Gammon

1. First, make the sauce. Melt the butter with the oil in a saucepan. Add the shallots, garlic and celery and cook over a low heat, stirring occasionally, for 5 minutes, until softened. Stir in the tomatoes, tomato purée, sugar to taste, parsley and wine and season to taste with salt and pepper. Increase the heat to medium and bring to the boil, then reduce the heat and simmer, stirring occasionally, for 15–20 minutes, until thickened.

2. Meanwhile, preheat the grill. Bring a large saucepan of lightly salted water to the boil. Add the pasta, bring back to the boil and cook for 8–10 minutes, until tender but still firm to the bite. Rub the gammon steaks with the sage and cook under the preheated grill for 6–7 minutes on each side, until tender and cooked through.

3. Drain the pasta, tip into a warmed serving dish and toss with the butter. Put the gammon steaks on top and pour the tomato sauce over them. Sprinkle with the olives and serve immediately.

Serves 4

225 g/8 oz dried tagliatelle verde

4 thick gammon steaks

1 tsp dried sage

25 g/1 oz butter

8 black olives, stoned and halved

salt

Tomato sauce

25 g/1 oz butter

2 tbsp olive oil

2 shallots, finely chopped

2 garlic cloves, finely chopped

1 celery stick, finely chopped

400 g/14 oz canned chopped tomatoes

2 tbsp tomato purée

brown sugar, to taste

1 tbsp chopped fresh flat-leaf parsley

100 ml/3½ fl oz dry white wine

salt and pepper

5

Ham & Asparagus Rolls in Sun-dried Tomato Sauce

1. First, make the sauce. Melt the butter with the oil in a saucepan. Add the shallots and celery and cook over a low heat, stirring occasionally, for 5 minutes, until softened. Stir in the fresh and sun-dried tomatoes, sun-dried tomato paste, sugar to taste, basil, olives and water and season to taste with salt and pepper. Increase the heat to medium and bring to the boil, then reduce the heat and simmer, stirring occasionally, for 15–20 minutes, until thickened.

2. Meanwhile, preheat the oven to 180°C/350°C/Gas Mark 4. Divide the asparagus spears equally among the slices of ham. Roll up the ham and put the rolls, seam-side down, into a large ovenproof dish.

3. Pour the tomato sauce over the ham rolls, sprinkle with the Parmesan and bake in the preheated oven for 20 minutes. Serve immediately.

Serves 6

850 g/1 lb 14 oz canned asparagus spears, drained

12 slices cooked ham

55 g/2 oz Parmesan cheese, grated

Sun-dried tomato sauce

* 25 g/1 oz butter
* 2 tbsp olive oil

2 shallots, finely chopped

* 1 celery stick, finely chopped
* 500 g/1 lb 2 oz plum tomatoes, peeled, cored and chopped

12 sun-dried tomatoes in oil, drained and chopped

2 tbsp sun-dried tomato paste

* brown sugar, to taste
* 1 tbsp chopped fresh basil

55 g/2 oz black olives, stoned and sliced

* 100 ml/3½ fl oz water
* salt and pepper

Chicken Croquettes in Rich Tomato Sauce

1. Heat half the oil in a saucepan. Add the onion and celery and cook over a low heat, stirring occasionally, for 5 minutes, until softened. Add the chicken, tomatoes and potatoes and cook, stirring frequently, for 8–10 minutes. Transfer the mixture to a food processor and process until smooth. Scrape into a bowl and leave to cool, then chill for 1 hour.

2. Meanwhile, make the sauce. Remove the bacon rind and dice the bacon. Melt the butter with the bacon rind in a saucepan. Add the bacon, shallot, garlic, celery and carrot and cook over a low heat, stirring occasionally, for 5 minutes. Stir in the tomatoes and cook, stirring occasionally, for 5 minutes. Stir the cornflour into the stock and pour it into the pan. Season to taste with salt and pepper. Cover and simmer, stirring occasionally, for 20 minutes, until thickened. Remove and discard the bacon rind.

3. Lightly dust your hands with flour and divide the chicken mixture into 8–12 pieces. Roll each into a small croquette. Place the eggs in a shallow bowl and spread out the breadcrumbs in a separate shallow bowl. Dip the croquettes into the beaten egg, then into the breadcrumbs to coat.

4. Heat the remaining oil in a frying pan. Add the croquettes and cook over a medium heat, turning once, for 10 minutes. Drain on kitchen paper. Pour the sauce over the croquettes, sprinkle with the parsley and serve immediately.

Serves 4

6 tbsp olive oil

1 onion, finely chopped

1 celery stick, finely chopped

225 g/8 oz cooked chicken, finely chopped

3 tomatoes, chopped

550 g/1 lb 4 oz boiled potatoes, finely chopped

plain flour, for dusting

2 eggs, lightly beaten

115 g/4 oz dry breadcrumbs

1 tbsp chopped fresh parsley

Rich tomato sauce

1 rasher lean bacon

25 g/1 oz butter

1 shallot, finely chopped

1 garlic clove, finely chopped

1 celery stick, finely chopped

1 carrot, finely chopped

400 g/14 oz canned chopped tomatoes

2 tsp cornflour

300 ml/10 fl oz chicken stock

salt and pepper

Chicken & Aubergine Layers Baked in Tomato Sauce

1. Put the chicken between two sheets of clingfilm and beat until thin and even. Cut into 10-cm/4-inch pieces and set aside.

2. To make the sauce, melt the butter with the oil in a saucepan. Add the onion, garlic and celery and cook over a low heat, stirring occasionally, for 5 minutes, until softened. Stir in the tomatoes, tomato purée, olives, sugar to taste, oregano and water and season to taste with salt and pepper. Increase the heat to medium and bring to the boil, then reduce the heat and simmer, stirring occasionally, for 15–20 minutes, until thickened.

3. Meanwhile, dip the aubergine slices in the flour to coat. Heat 5 tablespoons of the oil in a large frying pan and cook the aubergine slices, in batches, for 3 minutes on each side, until lightly browned, adding more oil as necessary.

4. Preheat the oven to 180°C/350°F/Gas Mark 4. Spread out the breadcrumbs in a shallow dish and lightly beat the egg in a separate shallow dish. Dip the chicken first in the egg and then in the breadcrumbs to coat. Heat the remaining oil in the frying pan. Add the chicken and cook over a medium heat for 2 minutes on each side, until golden.

5. Layer the chicken and aubergine slices in an ovenproof dish, pour over the sauce and sprinkle with the Parmesan. Bake in the preheated oven for 20 minutes, until golden. Garnish with parsley and serve immediately.

Serves 4

4 skinless, boneless chicken breasts

2 aubergines, sliced

4 tbsp plain flour

275 ml/9½ fl oz olive oil

55 g/2 oz dry breadcrumbs

1 egg

55 g/2 oz Parmesan cheese, grated

chopped fresh flat-leaf parsley, to garnish

Tomato sauce

✳ 25 g/1 oz butter

✳ 2 tbsp olive oil

✳ 1 onion, finely chopped

✳ 2 garlic cloves, finely chopped

✳ 1 celery stick, finely chopped

✳ 400 g/14 oz canned chopped tomatoes

✳ 2 tbsp tomato purée

6 stoned olives, sliced

✳ brown sugar, to taste

✳ 1 tsp dried oregano

✳ 100 ml/3½ fl oz water

✳ salt and pepper

10

Spaghetti with Tomato & Anchovy Sauce

1. First, make the sauce. Melt the butter with the oil in a saucepan. Add the shallots, garlic and celery and cook over a low heat, stirring occasionally, for 5 minutes, until softened. Stir in the tomatoes, tomato purée, sugar to taste, parsley, oregano, anchovies and water and season to taste with pepper. Increase the heat to medium and bring to the boil, then reduce the heat and simmer, stirring occasionally, for 30 minutes, until thickened.

2. Meanwhile, bring a large saucepan of lightly salted water to the boil. Add the spaghetti, bring back to the boil and cook for 8–10 minutes, until tender but still firm to the bite. Drain and tip into a warmed serving dish.

3. Taste the sauce and adjust the seasoning, adding salt and pepper if needed. Pour the sauce over the pasta and toss well. Garnish with parsley and serve immediately.

Serves 4

450 g/1 lb dried spaghetti
salt

Tomato & anchovy sauce
* 25 g/1 oz butter
* 2 tbsp olive oil
* 2 shallots, finely chopped
* 2 garlic cloves, finely chopped
* 1 celery stick, finely chopped
* 400 g/14 oz canned chopped tomatoes
* 2 tbsp tomato purée
* brown sugar, to taste
* 1 tbsp chopped fresh flat-leaf parsley, plus extra to garnish
* pinch of dried oregano
* 8 canned anchovy fillets, drained and chopped
* 100 ml/3½ fl oz water
* salt and pepper

Baked Trout in Tomato Sauce

1. First, make the sauce. Melt the butter with the oil in a saucepan. Add the onion, garlic and celery and cook over a low heat, stirring occasionally, for 5 minutes, until softened. Stir in the tomatoes, tomato purée, sugar to taste and water and season to taste with salt and pepper. Increase the heat to medium and bring to the boil, then reduce the heat and simmer, stirring occasionally, for 15–20 minutes, until thickened.

2. Meanwhile, preheat the oven to 180°C/350°F/Gas Mark 4. Spread out the flour in a shallow dish and season to taste with salt and pepper. Add the trout, one at a time, and turn to coat well in the flour, then shake off any excess.

3. Heat the oil in a flameproof casserole. Add the fish and cook over a medium heat for 3–4 minutes on each side, until lightly browned. Pour the tomato sauce over the fish, cover and bake in the preheated oven for 10–15 minutes, until the flesh flakes easily. Sprinkle with the parsley and serve immediately.

Serves 4

55 g/2 oz plain flour
4 whole trout, cleaned
3 tbsp olive oil
1 tbsp chopped fresh parsley
salt and pepper

Tomato sauce
* 25 g/1 oz butter
* 2 tbsp olive oil
* 1 onion, finely chopped
* 3 garlic cloves, finely chopped
* 2 celery sticks, finely chopped
* 1 kg/2 lb 4 oz plum tomatoes, peeled, cored and chopped
* 4 tbsp tomato purée
* brown sugar, to taste
* 100 ml/3½ fl oz water
* salt and pepper

Sole with Tomato Sauce

1. First, make the sauce. Melt the butter with the oil in a saucepan. Add the onion, garlic and celery and cook over a low heat, stirring occasionally, for 5 minutes, until softened. Stir in the tomatoes, tomato purée, sugar to taste, parsley and water and season to taste with salt and pepper. Increase the heat to medium and bring to the boil, then reduce the heat and simmer, stirring occasionally, for 20 minutes, until thickened.

2. Meanwhile, preheat the oven to 180°C/350°F/Gas Mark 4. Trim the sides of the fish fillets to make them straight, reserving the trimmings, then cut them in half lengthways. Season to taste with salt and pepper and sprinkle with the lemon juice.

3. Lightly beat the ricotta in a bowl with a fork until smooth. Chop the fish trimmings and stir them into the ricotta with the Tabasco. Spread the mixture over the strips of fish and roll up. Put the rolls into an ovenproof dish, seam-side down, in a single layer. Pour the stock over them and bake in the preheated oven for 20 minutes, until the fish flakes easily.

4. Using a slotted spoon, carefully transfer the fish rolls to a warmed serving dish. Spoon the tomato sauce over them and sprinkle over the olives and gherkin. Serve immediately.

Serves 4

4 large sole fillets, skinned

2 tbsp lemon juice

55 g/2 oz ricotta cheese

dash of Tabasco sauce

300 ml/10 fl oz fish stock

4 black olives, stoned and halved

1 pickled gherkin, chopped

salt and pepper

Tomato sauce

* 25 g/1 oz butter
* 2 tbsp olive oil
* 1 onion, finely chopped
* 2 garlic cloves, finely chopped
* 1 celery stick, finely chopped
* 400 g/14 oz canned chopped tomatoes
* 2 tbsp tomato purée
* brown sugar, to taste
* 1 tbsp chopped fresh flat-leaf parsley
* 100 ml/3½ fl oz water
* salt and pepper

Breaded Swordfish with Tomato & Courgette Sauce

1. First, make the sauce. Melt the butter with the oil in a large saucepan. Add the onion, garlic, celery and courgettes and cook over a low heat, stirring occasionally, for 8–10 minutes, until lightly browned. Stir in the tomatoes, tomato purée, capers, cayenne pepper and water and season to taste with salt and pepper. Increase the heat to medium and bring to the boil, then reduce the heat and simmer, stirring occasionally, for 15 minutes, until thickened.

2. Meanwhile, cut the fish steaks in half. Mix together the breadcrumbs and oregano in a shallow dish and lightly beat the eggs in a separate shallow dish. Dip the pieces of swordfish first into the eggs and then into breadcrumb mixture to coat.

3. Melt the butter in a large frying pan. Add the pieces of fish and cook over a medium heat, turning occasionally, for 6–8 minutes, until lightly browned.

4. Transfer the pieces of fish to the saucepan and spoon the sauce over them. Simmer, gently stirring occasionally, for 15 minutes, until the fish flakes easily. Transfer to a warmed serving dish and serve immediately.

Serves 4

4 swordfish steaks,
   about 225 g/8 oz each

85 g/3 oz dry breadcrumbs

1 tsp dried oregano

2 eggs

55 g/2 oz butter

Tomato & courgette sauce
* 25 g/1 oz butter
* 2 tbsp olive oil

1 Spanish onion, finely chopped
* 2 garlic cloves, finely chopped
* 1 celery stick, finely chopped

3 courgettes, cut into 5-mm/¼-inch slices
* 400 g/14 oz canned chopped tomatoes
* 2 tbsp tomato purée

1 tbsp drained capers

pinch of cayenne pepper
* 100 ml/3½ fl oz water
* salt and pepper

14

Prawns & Feta in Tomato Sauce

1. First, make the sauce. Melt the butter with the oil in a saucepan. Add the onion, garlic and celery and cook over a low heat, stirring occasionally, for 5 minutes, until softened. Stir in the tomatoes, tomato purée, sugar to taste, herbs and water. Increase the heat to medium and bring to the boil, then reduce the heat and simmer, stirring occasionally, for 15 minutes.

2. Stir in the wine and season to taste with salt and pepper. Increase the heat and bring to the boil, then reduce the heat and simmer, stirring occasionally, for a further 30 minutes, until thickened.

3. Stir in the prawns and feta cheese and cook, stirring frequently, for 5–8 minutes, until the prawns are cooked and the cheese has melted. Remove and discard the bay leaf. Transfer to a warmed serving dish and serve immediately.

Serves 4

500 g/1 lb 2 oz raw tiger prawns, peeled and deveined

85 g/3 oz feta cheese, crumbled

Tomato sauce

* 25 g/1 oz butter
* 2 tbsp olive oil
* 1 onion, finely chopped
* 3 garlic cloves, finely chopped
* 1 celery stick, finely chopped
* 1 kg/2 lb 4 oz plum tomatoes, peeled, cored and chopped
* 2 tbsp tomato purée
* brown sugar, to taste
* 1 tbsp chopped fresh flat-leaf parsley
* 1 fresh basil sprig, chopped
* 1 bay leaf
* ½ tsp dried oregano
* 100 ml/3½ fl oz water
* 225 ml/8 fl oz dry white wine
* salt and pepper

Succulent Tomato Shellfish

1. First, make the sauce. Melt the butter with the oil in a large saucepan. Add the shallot, garlic and celery and cook over a low heat, stirring occasionally, for 5 minutes, until softened. Stir in the tomatoes, tomato purée, sugar to taste, parsley and wine and season to taste with salt and pepper. Increase the heat to medium and bring to the boil, then reduce the heat and simmer, stirring occasionally, for 15–20 minutes, until thickened.

2. Meanwhile, scrub the mussels and clams under cold running water and pull off the beards from the mussels. Discard any with broken shells and any that refuse to close when tapped.

3. When the sauce has thickened, increase the heat and bring to the boil. Add the mussels and clams, cover and cook, gently shaking the pan occasionally, for 3–5 minutes, until the shells have opened. Discard any mussels and clams that remain closed. Transfer to a warmed serving dish, garnish with parsley and serve immediately.

Serves 4–6

1 kg/2 lb 4 oz live mussels
1 kg/2 lb 4 oz live clams

Tomato sauce
* 15 g/½ oz butter
* 1 tbsp olive oil
  1 shallot, finely chopped
* 1 garlic clove, finely chopped
* ½ celery stick, finely chopped
* 250 g/9 oz plum tomatoes, peeled, cored and chopped
* 1 tbsp tomato purée
* brown sugar, to taste
* 1 tbsp chopped fresh flat-leaf parsley, plus extra to garnish
  3 tbsp dry white wine
* salt and pepper

Tomato Soup

1. Melt the butter with the oil in a saucepan. Add the onion, garlic and celery and cook over a low heat, stirring occasionally, for 5 minutes, until softened. Stir in the tomatoes, tomato purée and water. Increase the heat to medium and bring to the boil, then reduce the heat and simmer, stirring occasionally, for 10 minutes.

2. Increase the heat to medium, then stir in sugar to taste, the basil and stock. Season to taste with salt and pepper. Bring to the boil, then reduce the heat and simmer for a further 10 minutes.

3. Taste and adjust the seasoning, adding salt and pepper if needed. Ladle into warmed bowls, garnish with basil and serve immediately.

Serves 4

* 25 g/1 oz butter
* 2 tbsp olive oil
* 1 large onion, finely chopped
* 2 garlic cloves, finely chopped
* 1 celery stick, finely chopped
* 500 g/1 lb 2 oz plum tomatoes, peeled, cored and chopped
* 2 tbsp tomato purée
* 100 ml/3½ fl oz water
* brown sugar, to taste
* 1 tbsp chopped fresh basil, plus extra to garnish
  300 ml/10 fl oz vegetable stock
* salt and pepper

French Beans Spanish-style

1. Melt the butter with the oil in a large saucepan. Add the shallots, garlic and celery and cook over a low heat, stirring occasionally, for 5 minutes, until softened. Add the beans and cook, stirring occasionally, for a further 4 minutes.

2. Stir in the tomatoes, tomato purée, sugar to taste, chives, bay leaf, pine kernels and lemon juice and season to taste with salt and pepper. Increase the heat to medium and bring to the boil, stirring constantly, then reduce the heat and simmer, stirring occasionally, for 25–30 minutes, until the beans are tender and the sauce has thickened.

3. Remove and discard the bay leaf. Transfer the mixture to a warmed serving dish, garnish with chives and serve immediately.

Serves 6

* 25 g/1 oz butter
* 2 tbsp olive oil
  2 shallots, finely chopped
* 2 garlic cloves, finely chopped
* 1 celery stick, finely chopped
  1 kg/2 lb 4 oz French beans, cut into 2.5-cm/1-inch lengths
* 800 g/1 lb 12 oz canned chopped tomatoes
* 2 tbsp tomato purée
* brown sugar, to taste
* 1 tbsp snipped fresh chives, plus extra to garnish
* 1 bay leaf
  1 tbsp chopped pine kernels
  1 tbsp lemon juice
* salt and pepper

Omelette Slices in Tomato & Red Wine Sauce

1. First, make the sauce. Melt the butter with the oil in a saucepan. Add the onion, garlic and celery and cook over a low heat, stirring occasionally, for 5 minutes, until softened. Stir in the tomatoes, tomato purée, sugar to taste, basil and wine and season to taste with salt and pepper. Increase the heat to medium and bring to the boil, then reduce the heat and simmer, stirring occasionally, for 15–20 minutes, until thickened.

2. Meanwhile, lightly beat the eggs in a bowl and season to taste with salt and pepper. Melt the butter with the oil in a 25-cm/10-inch frying pan over a medium heat. Pour in the eggs and tilt and rotate the pan to spread them evenly over the base of the pan. Cook for a few seconds, until the base of the omelette begins to set. Lift the edge with a palette knife and tilt the pan so that the uncooked egg runs underneath. Continue to cook until the base has set and the top is just firm but still creamy. Slide the omelette out of the pan onto a plate.

3. Cut the omelette into thick slices and transfer to a warmed serving dish. Strain the sauce over the omelette slices, turning them so that they are well coated. Garnish with basil and serve immediately.

Serves 4

8 eggs
15 g/½ oz butter
1 tbsp olive oil
salt and pepper

Tomato & red wine sauce
* 25 g/1 oz butter
* 2 tbsp olive oil
* 1 small onion, finely chopped
* 2 garlic cloves, finely chopped
* 1 celery stick, finely chopped
* 500 g/1 lb 2 oz plum tomatoes, peeled, cored and chopped
* 2 tbsp tomato purée
* brown sugar, to taste
* 1 tbsp chopped fresh basil, plus extra to garnish
  100 ml/3½ fl oz red wine
* salt and pepper

Penne in Tomato Sauce with Two Cheeses

1. First, make the sauce. Melt the butter with the oil in a saucepan. Add the shallots, garlic and celery and cook over a low heat, stirring occasionally, for 5 minutes, until softened. Stir in the tomatoes, tomato purée, sugar to taste, oregano and water and season to taste with salt and pepper. Increase the heat to medium and bring to the boil, then reduce the heat and simmer, stirring occasionally, for 15–20 minutes, until thickened.

2. Meanwhile, bring a large saucepan of lightly salted water to the boil. Add the pasta, bring back to the boil and cook for 8–10 minutes, until tender but still firm to the bite. Drain and return to the pan.

3. Add the tomato sauce and the cheeses to the pasta and toss well over a very low heat until the cheeses have melted. Transfer to a warmed serving dish and serve immediately.

Serves 4

450 g/1 lb dried penne

115 g/4 oz Bel Paese cheese, diced

55 g/2 oz Parmesan cheese, grated

salt

Tomato sauce

* 25 g/1 oz butter
* 2 tbsp olive oil
* 2 shallots, finely chopped
* 2 garlic cloves, finely chopped
* 1 celery stick, finely chopped
* 400 g/14 oz canned chopped tomatoes
* 2 tbsp tomato purée
* brown sugar, to taste
* 1 tsp dried oregano
* 100 ml/3½ fl oz water
* salt and pepper

Baked Eggs with Tomato & Sweetcorn Sauce

1. Melt the butter with the oil in a saucepan. Add the onion, garlic and celery and cook over a low heat, stirring occasionally, for 5 minutes, until softened. Add the bacon and red pepper and cook, stirring occasionally, for a further 10 minutes. Stir in the tomatoes, tomato purée, sugar to taste, parsley, cayenne and water and season to taste with salt and pepper. Increase the heat to medium and bring to the boil, then reduce the heat and simmer, stirring occasionally, for 15 minutes, until thickened.

2. Meanwhile, preheat the oven to 180°C/350°F/Gas Mark 4. Stir the sweetcorn into the sauce and transfer the mixture to an ovenproof dish. Make four small hollows with the back of a spoon and break an egg into each. Bake in the preheated oven for 25–30 minutes, until the eggs have set. Serve immediately.

Serves 4

* 25 g/1 oz butter
* 2 tbsp olive oil
* 1 onion, finely chopped
* 2 garlic cloves, finely chopped
* 1 celery stick, finely chopped
* 225 g/8 oz lean bacon, diced
* 1 red pepper, deseeded and diced
* 500 g/1 lb 2 oz plum tomatoes, peeled, cored and chopped
* 2 tbsp tomato purée
* brown sugar, to taste
* 1 tbsp chopped fresh parsley
* pinch of cayenne pepper
* 100 ml/3½ fl oz water
* 225 g/8 oz canned sweetcorn, drained
* 4 large eggs
* salt and pepper

Griddled Halloumi with Tomato Yogurt Sauce

1. First, make the sauce. Melt the butter with the oil in a saucepan. Add the onion and garlic and cook over a low heat, stirring occasionally, for 5 minutes, until softened. Stir in the tomatoes, tomato purée, sugar to taste and water and season to taste with salt and pepper. Increase the heat to medium and bring to the boil, then reduce the heat and simmer, stirring occasionally, for 15–20 minutes, until thickened. Remove the pan from the heat and leave the sauce to cool.

2. When the sauce is cold, stir in the cumin, coriander and yogurt and set aside. Make a bed of lettuce on each of four serving plates.

3. Cut the cheese into 16 slices. Heat a griddle pan. Cook the cheese slices for 3–4 minutes on each side, then divide them among the plates. Spoon the tomato yogurt sauce onto the plates, sprinkle with the olives and serve immediately.

Serves 4

350 g/12 oz halloumi cheese
85 g/3 oz stoned black olives
shredded lettuce, to serve

Tomato yogurt sauce
* 25 g/1 oz butter
* 2 tbsp olive oil
* 1 small onion, finely chopped
* 2 garlic cloves, finely chopped
* 500 g/1 lb 2 oz plum tomatoes, peeled, cored and chopped
* 2 tbsp tomato purée
* brown sugar, to taste
* 100 ml/3½ fl oz water
  1 tbsp ground cumin
  1 tbsp ground coriander
  150 ml/5 fl oz natural yogurt
* salt and pepper

Courgette, Pepper & Tomato Gratin

1. Melt the butter with the oil in a large saucepan. Add the onion, garlic, celery, courgettes and peppers and cook over a low heat, stirring occasionally, for 5 minutes, until softened. Stir in the tomatoes, tomato purée, sugar to taste, basil, bay leaf and water and season to taste with salt and pepper. Increase the heat to medium and bring to the boil, then reduce the heat and simmer, stirring occasionally, for 30 minutes, until thickened and the vegetables are tender.

2. Meanwhile, preheat the grill. Remove and discard the bay leaf and spoon the vegetable mixture into a flameproof dish. Sprinkle with the anchovies and Parmesan and cook under the preheated grill for 3–5 minutes, until the top is golden brown and bubbling. Serve immediately.

Serves 4

* 25 g/1 oz butter
* 2 tbsp olive oil
* 1 onion, thinly sliced
* 2 garlic cloves, finely chopped
* 1 celery stick, finely chopped
* 700 g/1 lb 9 oz courgettes, sliced
* 2 large red peppers, deseeded and sliced
* 400 g/14 oz canned chopped tomatoes
* 2 tbsp tomato purée
* brown sugar, to taste
* 1 tbsp chopped fresh basil
* 1 bay leaf
* 100 ml/3½ fl oz water
* 6 canned anchovy fillets, drained and chopped
* 55 g/2 oz Parmesan cheese, grated
* salt and pepper

Favourite

23

Lasagne

① Heat the oil in a large saucepan. Add the pancetta and cook over a medium heat, stirring occasionally, for 2–3 minutes. Reduce the heat to low, add the garlic and onion and cook, stirring occasionally, for 5 minutes, until softened.

② Add the beef, increase the heat to medium and cook, stirring frequently and breaking it up with the spoon, for 8–10 minutes, until evenly browned. Stir in the carrots, celery and mushrooms and cook, stirring occasionally, for a further 5 minutes. Add the oregano, pour in the wine and stock and stir in the sun-dried tomato paste. Season to taste with salt and pepper. Bring to the boil, reduce the heat and simmer for 40 minutes.

③ Preheat the oven to 190°C/375°F/Gas Mark 5. Make alternating layers of the beef sauce, lasagne sheets and Parmesan in a large, rectangular ovenproof dish. Pour the tomato sauce over the top to cover completely. Bake in the preheated oven for 30 minutes. Remove the dish from the oven and leave to stand for 10 minutes, then cut into squares and serve with a mixed salad.

Serves 4

2 tbsp olive oil

55 g/2 oz pancetta or bacon, chopped

1 garlic clove, finely chopped

1 onion, chopped

225 g/8 oz fresh beef mince

2 carrots, chopped

2 celery sticks, chopped

115 g/4 oz mushrooms, chopped

pinch of dried oregano

5 tbsp red wine

150 ml/5 fl oz beef stock

1 tbsp sun-dried tomato paste

225 g/8 oz dried no-precook lasagne sheets

115 g/4 oz Parmesan cheese, grated

✳ 1 quantity Basic Tomato Sauce (see page 10)

salt and pepper

mixed salad, to serve

24

Spaghetti & Meatballs in Tomato Sauce

1. Tear the bread into pieces and place into a large bowl. Pour over the milk and leave to soak for 5 minutes. Add the beef, garlic, breadcrumbs, 5 tablespoons of the Parmesan, the egg, lemon rind and thyme. Season to taste with salt and pepper, then mix well with your hands until thoroughly combined. Shape the mixture into about 30 walnut-sized balls and put them on a baking sheet. Chill in the refrigerator for 30 minutes.

2. Meanwhile, pour the tomato sauce into a large saucepan and place over a low heat. Heat gently until warmed through.

3. Melt 115 g/4 oz of the butter in a frying pan. Add the meatballs, in batches, and cook over a medium heat, turning occasionally, for 6–8 minutes, until evenly browned. Using a slotted spoon, transfer the meatballs to the tomato sauce. When they have all been added, cover the pan and simmer for 25–30 minutes, until cooked through.

4. Meanwhile, bring a large pan of salted water to the boil. Add the spaghetti, bring back to the boil and cook for 8–10 minutes, until tender but still firm to the bite. Drain, tip into a warmed serving dish and toss with the remaining butter. Spoon the meatballs on top and pour the sauce over them. Sprinkle with the remaining Parmesan and serve immediately.

Serves 4

2 thick slices bread, crusts removed

3 tbsp milk

1 kg/2 lb 4 oz fresh beef mince

3 garlic cloves, finely chopped

25 g/1 oz dry breadcrumbs

85 g/3 oz Parmesan cheese

1 egg, lightly beaten

2 tsp grated lemon rind

1 tsp dried thyme

1 quantity Basic Tomato Sauce (see page 10)

150 g/5½ oz butter

500 g/1 lb 2 oz dried spaghetti

salt and pepper

Veal Schnitzel with Tomato & Bitter Orange Sauce

1. Put the escalopes between two sheets of clingfilm and beat with a meat mallet or the side of a rolling pin until thin and even. Transfer to a shallow dish, sprinkle with the lemon juice and salt and pepper to taste. Cover with clingfilm and leave to marinate for 1 hour.

2. Meanwhile, make the sauce. Cut the orange rind into thin shreds and set aside. Melt the butter with the oil in a saucepan. Add the shallots, garlic and celery and cook over a low heat, stirring occasionally, for 5 minutes, until softened. Stir the tomatoes, tomato purée, sugar to taste, orange juice and most the orange rind into the pan and season to taste with salt and pepper. Increase the heat to medium and bring to the boil, then reduce the heat and simmer, stirring occasionally, for 15–20 minutes, until thickened.

3. Lightly beat the egg in a shallow dish and spread out the breadcrumbs in a separate shallow dish. Dip the escalopes first in the egg and then in the breadcrumbs to coat.

4. Melt the butter in a frying pan. Add two escalopes and cook for 3–4 minutes on each side, until golden brown and cooked through. Remove from the pan and keep warm while you cook the remaining escalopes. Transfer the escalopes to a warmed serving dish. Pour the sauce over them and garnish with parsley sprigs and the remaining orange rind. Serve immediately.

Serves 4

4 veal escalopes
juice of 2 lemons
1 large egg
115 g/4 oz dry breadcrumbs
50 g/1¾ oz butter
salt and pepper
fresh flat-leaf parsley sprigs,
    to garnish

Tomato & bitter orange sauce
thinly pared rind and juice of
    2 Seville oranges (use
    regular oranges if Seville
    oranges are unavailable)
* 25 g/1 oz butter
* 2 tbsp olive oil
  2 shallots, finely chopped
* 2 garlic cloves, finely chopped
* 1 celery stick, finely chopped
* 500 g/1 lb 2 oz plum tomatoes,
    peeled, cored and chopped
* 2 tbsp tomato purée
* brown sugar, to taste
* salt and pepper

Hawaiian Pizza

1. To make the pizza dough, sift the flour and salt into a bowl and stir in the yeast. Make a well in the centre and pour in the oil and lukewarm water, then mix to a soft dough. Turn out onto a lightly floured surface and knead for 10 minutes, until smooth and elastic. Shape into a ball, put it into an oiled plastic bag and leave to rise in a warm place for about 1 hour, until doubled in volume.

2. Melt the butter with the oil in a saucepan. Add the onion and celery and cook over a low heat, stirring occasionally, for 5 minutes, until softened. Stir in the tomatoes, tomato purée, sugar to taste, oregano and water and season to taste with salt and pepper. Increase the heat to medium and bring to the boil, then reduce the heat and simmer, stirring occasionally, for 15–20 minutes, until thickened. Remove from the heat and set aside.

3. Preheat the oven to 220°C/425°F/Gas Mark 7. Brush a baking sheet with oil. Knock back the dough and knead briefly on a lightly floured surface. Roll out into a round and transfer to the prepared baking sheet. Push up a rim all the way around.

4. Spread the tomato sauce evenly over the pizza base. Sprinkle evenly with the ham and pineapple, then top with the cheese. Drizzle with oil and bake in the preheated oven for 15–20 minutes, until crisp and golden. Serve immediately.

Serves 2

* 15 g/½ oz butter
* 1 tbsp olive oil, plus extra for brushing and drizzling
* 1 small onion, finely chopped
* ½ celery stick, finely chopped
* 200 g/7 oz canned chopped tomatoes
* 1 tbsp tomato purée
* brown sugar, to taste
* ½ tsp dried oregano
* 3 tbsp water
* 175 g/6 oz ham, diced
* 225 g/8 oz canned pineapple chunks in juice, drained
* 55 g/2 oz Cheddar cheese, grated
* salt and pepper

Pizza dough
225 g/8 oz strong white flour, plus extra for dusting

1 tsp salt

½ tsp easy-blend dried yeast

1 tbsp olive oil

150 ml/5 fl oz lukewarm water

27

Chicago Pizza

1. Melt the butter with the oil in a saucepan. Add the onion, garlic and celery and cook over a low heat, stirring occasionally, for 5 minutes, until softened. Stir in the canned tomatoes, tomato purée, honey, Worcestershire sauce, vinegar, mustard powder and Tabasco and season to taste with salt and pepper. Increase the heat to medium and bring to the boil, then reduce the heat and simmer, stirring occasionally, for 15–20 minutes, until thickened. Remove from the heat and set aside.

2. Preheat the oven to 220°C/425°F/Gas Mark 7. Brush a baking sheet with oil. Knock back the dough and knead briefly on a lightly floured surface. Roll out into a round and transfer to the prepared baking sheet. Push up a rim all the way around.

3. Spread the tomato sauce evenly over the pizza base and top with the tomato slices. Sprinkle with the ham, cover with the pepperoni and top with the chillies. Sprinkle with the cheese, drizzle with oil and bake in the preheated oven for 15–20 minutes, until crisp and golden. Serve immediately.

Serves 2

* 15 g/½ oz butter
* 1 tbsp olive oil, plus extra for brushing and drizzling
* 1 small onion, finely chopped
* 1 garlic clove, finely chopped
* 1 celery stick, finely chopped
* 200 g/7 oz canned chopped tomatoes
* 1 tbsp tomato purée
  1½ tbsp clear honey
  1 tbsp Worcestershire sauce
  1½ tsp white wine vinegar
  ½ tsp mustard powder
  dash of Tabasco sauce
  1 quantity Pizza Dough (see page 66)
  plain flour, for dusting
  4 tomatoes, sliced
  100 g/3½ oz smoked ham, diced
  115 g/4 oz pepperoni, thinly sliced
  2 fresh red chillies, thinly sliced
  55 g/2 oz Cheddar cheese, grated
* salt and pepper

Spare Ribs in Barbecue Sauce

1. Preheat the oven to 200°C/400°F/Gas Mark 6. Melt the butter with the oil in a saucepan. Add the onion, garlic and celery and cook over a low heat, stirring occasionally, for 5 minutes, until softened. Stir in the tomatoes, tomato purée, sugar, orange juice, honey, mustard, vinegar and Worcestershire sauce and season to taste with salt and pepper. Increase the heat to medium and bring to the boil, then reduce the heat and simmer, stirring occasionally, for 15–20 minutes, until thickened. Remove the pan from the heat.

2. Spread out the spare ribs in a shallow roasting tin and bake in the preheated oven for 25 minutes. Remove from the oven and spoon half the sauce over them. Reduce the oven temperature to 180°C/350°F/Gas Mark 4, return the tin to the oven and cook for a further 20 minutes.

3. Remove the tin from the oven and turn the ribs over. Spoon the remaining sauce over them and return the tin to the oven. Cook for a further 25–30 minutes, until the meat is tender. Garnish with parsley and serve immediately.

Serves 4

* 25 g/1 oz butter
* 2 tbsp olive oil
* 1 onion, finely chopped
* 2 garlic cloves, finely chopped
* 1 celery stick, finely chopped
* 400 g/14 oz canned chopped tomatoes
* 2 tbsp tomato purée
* 2–3 tbsp brown sugar
  2 tbsp orange juice
  1 tbsp clear honey
  1 tsp wholegrain mustard
  2 tbsp red wine vinegar
  1 tbsp Worcestershire sauce
  1.5 kg/3 lb 5 oz pork spare ribs
* salt and pepper
  chopped fresh flat-leaf parsley, to garnish

Italian Pork Escalopes

1 First, make the sauce. Melt the butter with the oil in a saucepan. Add the onion, garlic and celery and cook over a low heat, stirring occasionally, for 5 minutes, until softened. Stir in the tomatoes, tomato purée, sugar to taste, basil, bay leaf and wine and season to taste with salt and pepper. Increase the heat to medium and bring to the boil, then reduce the heat and simmer, stirring occasionally, for 15–20 minutes, until thickened.

2 Meanwhile, put the escalopes between two sheets of clingfilm and beat with a meat mallet or the side of a rolling pin until thin and even. Season well with pepper. Preheat the grill.

3 Heat the oil in a frying pan. Add two escalopes and cook over a medium–high heat for 1–1½ minutes on each side, until golden brown. Transfer to a large flameproof dish. Cook the remaining escalopes in the same way and transfer to the dish.

4 Remove and discard the bay leaf from the tomato sauce, then spread the sauce evenly over the escalopes. Sprinkle with the basil and top with the mozzarella cheese. Cook under the preheated grill for 1–2 minutes, until the cheese has melted. Serve immediately.

Serves 4

4 pork escalopes, about 115 g/4 oz each

2 tbsp olive oil

2 tbsp chopped fresh basil

85 g/3 oz mozzarella cheese, thinly sliced

pepper

Tomato sauce

25 g/1 oz butter

2 tbsp olive oil

1 red onion, finely chopped

2 garlic cloves, finely chopped

1 celery stick, finely chopped

400 g/14 oz canned chopped tomatoes

2 tbsp tomato purée

brown sugar, to taste

2 tbsp chopped fresh basil

1 bay leaf

100 ml/3½ fl oz dry white wine

salt and pepper

30

Gammon Steaks with Tomato & Sage Sauce

1. First, make the sauce. Melt the butter with the oil in a saucepan. Add the onions, garlic, celery and green pepper and cook over a low heat, stirring occasionally, for 5 minutes, until softened. Stir in the tomatoes, tomato purée, sugar to taste, fresh sage and water and season to taste with salt and pepper. Increase the heat to medium and bring to the boil, then reduce the heat and simmer, stirring occasionally, for 25–30 minutes, until thickened.

2. Preheat the grill. Season the gammon steaks with pepper to taste and rub with the dried sage. Cook under the preheated grill for 5 minutes on each side, until tender and cooked through. Transfer to warmed serving plates, spoon the sauce over them and serve immediately.

Serves 4

4 gammon steaks
1 tsp dried sage
pepper

Tomato & sage sauce
* 25 g/1 oz butter
* 2 tbsp olive oil
* 2 large onions, thinly sliced
* 2 garlic cloves, finely chopped
* 1 celery stick, finely chopped
* 1 green pepper, deseeded and cut into julienne strips
* 800 g/1 lb 12 oz canned chopped tomatoes
* 3 tbsp tomato purée
* brown sugar, to taste
* 1 tbsp chopped fresh sage
* 100 ml/3½ fl oz water
* salt and pepper

31

Cannelloni with Chicken & Ham

1. First, make the sauce. Melt the butter with the oil in a saucepan. Add the onion, garlic and celery and cook over a low heat, stirring occasionally, for 5 minutes, until softened. Stir in the tomatoes, tomato purée, sugar to taste, parsley and water and season to taste with salt and pepper. Increase the heat to medium and bring to the boil, then reduce the heat and simmer, stirring occasionally, for 20–30 minutes, until thickened.

2. Preheat the oven to 190°C/375°F/Gas Mark 5. Brush an ovenproof dish with oil. Heat the oil in a frying pan, add the onion and cook over a low heat, stirring occasionally, for 5 minutes, until softened. Add the chicken and cook, stirring frequently, for a further few minutes, until lightly browned. Remove the pan from the heat, stir in the ham and cream cheese and season to taste with salt and pepper.

3. Fill the cannelloni tubes with the chicken mixture and put them into the prepared dish. Pour the sauce over them, sprinkle with the Parmesan and bake in the preheated oven for 35–40 minutes. Serve immediately.

Serves 4

- 1 tbsp olive oil, plus extra for brushing
- 1 small onion, finely chopped
- 175 g/6 oz fresh chicken mince
- 115 g/4 oz ham, finely chopped
- 70 g/2½ oz cream cheese with garlic and herbs
- 8 dried no-precook cannelloni tubes
- 4 tbsp grated Parmesan cheese
- salt and pepper

Tomato sauce
- 25 g/1 oz butter
- 2 tbsp olive oil
- 1 onion, finely chopped
- 2 garlic cloves, finely chopped
- 1 celery stick, finely chopped
- 400 g/14 oz canned chopped tomatoes
- 2 tbsp tomato purée
- brown sugar, to taste
- 1 tbsp chopped fresh flat-leaf parsley
- 100 ml/3½ fl oz water
- salt and pepper

32

Barbecued Chicken

1. First, make the sauce. Melt the butter with the oil in a saucepan. Add the onion, garlic, celery and ginger and cook over a low heat, stirring occasionally, for 5 minutes, until softened. Stir in the tomatoes, tomato purée, Worcestershire sauce, vinegar, lemon juice, sugar, oregano, bay leaf, nutmeg and water and season to taste with salt and pepper. Increase the heat to medium and bring to the boil, then reduce the heat and simmer, stirring occasionally, for 30–40 minutes, until thickened.

2. Meanwhile, preheat the barbecue or grill. Brush the skin sides of the chicken halves with half the oil and put them skin-side down on the barbecue grill or skin-side uppermost on the grill rack. Cook over hot coals or under the preheated grill for 10 minutes, then brush with the remaining oil, turn them over and cook for a further 20 minutes, until golden brown.

3. Brush the chicken with half the sauce. Continue to cook, turning and brushing frequently with the remaining sauce, for 15–20 minutes, until cooked through and tender. Transfer to a warmed serving dish and serve immediately.

Serves 4

2 double poussins or spring chickens, about 900 g/ 2 lb each, cut in half

4 tbsp olive oil

Barbecue sauce
- 25 g/1 oz butter
- 2 tbsp olive oil
- 1 onion, finely chopped
- 2 garlic cloves, finely chopped
- 1 celery stick, finely chopped
- 1-cm/½-inch piece fresh ginger, finely chopped
- 400 g/14 oz canned chopped tomatoes
- 2 tbsp tomato purée
- 1 tbsp Worcestershire sauce
- 2 tbsp red wine vinegar
- 2 tbsp lemon juice
- 1 tbsp brown sugar
- 1 tsp dried oregano
- 1 bay leaf
- pinch of grated nutmeg
- 2 tbsp water
- salt and pepper

33

Chicken Goujons with Tomato & Honey Dipping Sauce

1. First, make the sauce. Melt the butter with the olive oil in a saucepan. Add the onion, garlic and celery and cook over a low heat, stirring occasionally, for 5 minutes, until softened. Stir in the tomatoes, tomato purée, cinnamon, ginger and water and season to taste with salt and pepper. Increase the heat to medium and bring to the boil, then reduce the heat and simmer, stirring occasionally, for 40–50 minutes, until very thick.

2. Meanwhile, put the chicken between two sheets of clingfilm and beat with a meat mallet or the side of a rolling pin until thin and even. Cut the chicken into 2.5 cm/1 inch wide strips. Mix together the breadcrumbs, coriander, cumin and turmeric in a shallow dish and season to taste with salt and pepper. Spread out the flour in a separate shallow dish and lightly beat the egg in a third dish. Toss the chicken strips, one at a time, first in the flour, then in the egg and, finally, in the breadcrumb mixture.

3. Heat enough groundnut oil for deep-frying in a deep-fat fryer to 180–190°C/350–375°F, or until a cube of bread browns in 30 seconds. Add the goujons to the hot oil, in batches, and cook until golden brown and crisp. Drain on kitchen paper and keep warm.

4. Stir the honey into the sauce and cook for 1 minute. Add the sesame seeds and pour the sauce into a small bowl. Serve the chicken goujons immediately with the sauce.

Serves 4

2 skinless, boneless chicken breasts, about 175 g/ 6 oz each

85 g/3 oz fresh breadcrumbs

½ tsp ground coriander

¼ tsp ground cumin

¼ tsp ground turmeric

2 tbsp plain flour

1 egg

groundnut oil, for deep-frying

salt and pepper

Tomato & honey sauce

25 g/1 oz butter

2 tbsp olive oil

1 onion, finely chopped

2 garlic cloves, finely chopped

1 celery stick, finely chopped

500 g/1 lb 2 oz plum tomatoes, peeled, cored and chopped

2 tbsp tomato purée

1 tsp ground cinnamon

pinch of ground ginger

100 ml/3½ fl oz water

2 tbsp clear honey

1 tsp toasted sesame seeds

salt and pepper

34

Turkey Escalopes with Tomato & Apple Sauce

1. First, make the sauce. Melt the butter with the olive oil in a saucepan. Add the shallots and apple and cook over a low heat, stirring occasionally, for 5 minutes, until softened. Stir in the tomatoes, tomato purée, sugar to taste, nutmeg and water and season to taste with salt and pepper. Increase the heat to medium and bring to the boil, then reduce the heat and simmer, stirring occasionally, for 15–20 minutes, until thickened. Remove the sauce from the heat and leave to cool slightly.

2. Put the turkey between two sheets of clingfilm and beat with a meat mallet or the side of a rolling pin until thin and even. Put the flour into a shallow dish and season to taste with salt and pepper. Lightly beat the egg in a separate shallow dish and spread out the breadcrumbs in a third shallow dish.

3. Dip the escalopes, one at a time, first in the flour, then in the egg and, finally, in the breadcrumbs to coat. Melt the butter with the sunflower oil in a large frying pan. Add the escalopes, in batches, and cook over a medium heat for 1 minute on each side, until golden brown. Reduce the heat and cook for a further 3–4 minutes on each side, until tender.

4. Meanwhile, gently reheat the sauce. Transfer the escalopes to warmed serving plates and pour the sauce over them. Garnish with parsley and serve immediately.

Serves 4

4 turkey escalopes
3 tbsp plain flour
1 egg
55 g/2 oz dry breadcrumbs
55 g/2 oz butter
2 tbsp sunflower oil
salt and pepper
chopped fresh flat-leaf parsley, to garnish

Tomato & apple sauce
* 25 g/1 oz butter
* 2 tbsp olive oil
  2 shallots, finely chopped
  1 eating apple, peeled, cored and diced
* 400 g/14 oz canned chopped tomatoes
* 2 tbsp tomato purée
* brown sugar, to taste
  pinch of grated nutmeg
* 100 ml/3½ fl oz water
* salt and pepper

35

Fish Baked in Tomato Sauce

1. First, make the sauce. Melt the butter with the oil in a saucepan. Add the shallots, garlic and celery and cook over a low heat, stirring occasionally, for 5 minutes, until softened. Stir in the tomatoes, tomato purée, sugar to taste, parsley and wine and season to taste with salt and pepper. Increase the heat to medium and bring to the boil, then reduce the heat and simmer, stirring occasionally, for 15–20 minutes, until thickened.

2. Meanwhile, preheat the oven to 190°C/375°F/Gas Mark 5. Grease an ovenproof dish with butter. Put the fish into the prepared dish in a single layer. Spoon the sauce over the fish steaks and sprinkle with the breadcrumbs.

3. Bake in the preheated oven, spooning the cooking juices over the fish 2–3 times, for 20–30 minutes, until the topping is crisp and golden brown. Serve.

Serves 4

butter, for greasing
4 white fish steaks
2 tbsp dry breadcrumbs

Tomato sauce
* 25 g/1 oz butter
* 2 tbsp olive oil
  2 shallots, finely chopped
* 2 garlic cloves, finely chopped
* 1 celery stick, finely chopped
* 400 g/14 oz canned chopped tomatoes
* 2 tbsp tomato purée
* brown sugar, to taste
* 2 tbsp chopped fresh parsley
  100 ml/3½ fl oz dry white wine
* salt and pepper

36

Crab Cakes with Rich Tomato Sauce

1. Peel both kinds of potatoes and cut into chunks. Cook in a large saucepan of salted boiling water for 15–20 minutes, until tender but not falling apart. Drain well, return to the pan and mash roughly, then leave to cool.

2. Stir the egg into the cooled potatoes, then stir in the crabmeat, flour, mustard powder and tarragon. Season to taste with salt and pepper. Lightly flour your hands, scoop up 2 tablespoons of the mixture and shape into a cake. Repeat, flouring your hands as required, until all the mixture has been used up. Put the crab cakes on a baking sheet and chill in the refrigerator for 30 minutes to firm up.

3. Meanwhile, make the sauce. Melt the butter with 2 tablespoons of oil from the jar of sun-dried tomatoes in a saucepan. Add the shallots, garlic and celery and cook over a low heat, stirring occasionally, for 5 minutes, until softened. Stir in the fresh tomatoes, sun-dried tomatoes, sun-dried tomato paste, sugar to taste, wine and tarragon. Season to taste with salt and pepper. Increase the heat to medium and bring to the boil, then reduce the heat and simmer, stirring occasionally, for 15–20 minutes, until thickened.

4. Heat the sunflower oil in a large frying pan. Add the crab cakes, in batches, and cook for 2–3 minutes on each side, until golden brown and heated through. Serve immediately with the sauce and lemon wedges for squeezing over.

Serves 4

225 g/8 oz potatoes

450 g/1 lb sweet potatoes

1 egg, lightly beaten

280 g/10 oz white crabmeat

2 tbsp plain flour, plus extra for dusting

1 tbsp mustard powder

2 tsp chopped fresh tarragon

4 tbsp sunflower oil

salt and pepper

lemon wedges, to serve

Rich tomato sauce

25 g/1 oz butter

4 sun-dried tomatoes in oil, drained and chopped

2 shallots, finely chopped

2 garlic cloves, finely chopped

1 celery stick, finely chopped

500 g/1 lb 2 oz plum tomatoes, peeled, cored and chopped

2 tbsp sun-dried tomato paste

brown sugar, to taste

100 ml/3½ fl oz dry white wine

1 tbsp chopped fresh tarragon

salt and pepper

37

Prawn Fritters with Roasted Tomato Sauce

1. If the prawns are very large, cut them in half. Put them into a bowl and sprinkle with the lemon juice and olive oil. Season to taste with salt and pepper and leave to marinate for 1 hour.

2. Meanwhile, make the batter. Sift the flour and salt into a bowl. Add the eggs and water and beat until smooth. Cover and set aside to rest.

3. Preheat the oven to 220°C/425°F/Gas Mark 7. To make the sauce, put the onion, garlic, tomatoes, sugar and vinegar into a large ovenproof dish and drizzle with the olive oil. Roast in the preheated oven, stirring occasionally, for 30–35 minutes, until the vegetables are soft.

4. Remove the dish from the oven and leave to cool slightly, then transfer to a food processor or blender and process until smooth. Scrape the sauce into a clean pan, stir in the parsley and season to taste with salt and pepper.

5. Stir the batter, then stir in the prawns. Heat enough groundnut oil for deep-frying in a deep-fat fryer to 170°C/340°F, or until a cube of bread browns in 1 minute. Meanwhile, gently reheat the sauce. Add spoonfuls of the prawn mixture to the hot oil and cook for 4–5 minutes, until crisp and golden brown. Remove with a slotted spoon and drain on kitchen paper. Transfer the prawn fritters to a warmed serving dish and pour the sauce into a serving bowl. Serve immediately.

Serves 4

500 g/1 lb 2 oz raw prawns, peeled and deveined
2 tbsp lemon juice
2 tbsp olive oil
groundnut oil, for deep-frying
salt and pepper

Batter

115 g/4 oz plain flour
pinch of salt
2 eggs
150 ml/5 fl oz water

Roasted tomato sauce

1 large onion, chopped
3 garlic cloves, chopped
500 g/1 lb 2 oz plum tomatoes, peeled, cored and chopped
2 tbsp brown sugar
2 tbsp red wine vinegar
2 tbsp olive oil
1 tbsp chopped fresh flat-leaf parsley
salt and pepper

Margherita Pizza

1. Melt the butter with the oil in a saucepan. Add the onion, garlic and celery and cook over a low heat, stirring occasionally, for 5 minutes, until softened. Stir in the canned tomatoes, tomato purée, sugar to taste, chopped basil and water and season to taste with salt and pepper. Increase the heat to medium and bring to the boil, then reduce the heat and simmer, stirring occasionally, for 15–20 minutes, until thickened. Remove from the heat and set aside.

2. Preheat the oven to 220°C/425°F/Gas Mark 7. Brush a baking sheet with oil. Knock back the dough and knead briefly on a lightly floured surface. Roll out into a round and transfer to the prepared baking sheet. Push up a rim all the way around.

3. Spread the tomato sauce evenly over the base. Arrange the mozzarella and tomato slices alternately on top. Coarsely tear the basil leaves and put them on the pizza, then sprinkle with the Parmesan. Drizzle with oil and bake in the preheated oven for 15–20 minutes, until crisp and golden. Serve immediately.

Serves 2

* 15 g/½ oz butter
* 1 tbsp olive oil, plus extra for brushing and drizzling
* 1 small onion, finely chopped
* 1 garlic clove, finely chopped
* ½ celery stick, finely chopped
* 200 g/7 oz canned chopped tomatoes
* 1 tbsp tomato purée
* brown sugar, to taste
* 1 tbsp chopped fresh basil
* 3 tbsp water
  1 quantity Pizza Dough (see page 66)
  plain flour, for dusting
  140 g/5 oz mozzarella cheese, sliced
  4 tomatoes, sliced
  1 fresh basil sprig
  2 tbsp grated Parmesan cheese
* salt and pepper

Vegetables à la Grecque

1. Melt the butter with the oil in a saucepan. Add the onion, garlic and celery and cook over a low heat, stirring occasionally, for 5 minutes, until softened. Stir in the tomatoes, tomato purée, sugar to taste, wine, lemon juice and parsley and season to taste with salt and pepper. Increase the heat to medium and bring to the boil, then reduce the heat and simmer, stirring occasionally, for 15–20 minutes, until thickened.

2. Add the shallots and cauliflower and simmer for 10 minutes, then stir in the mushrooms and simmer for a further 5 minutes.

3. Using a slotted spoon, transfer the shallots, cauliflower and mushrooms to a serving dish. Increase the heat to medium–high and cook the sauce, stirring constantly, until reduced and thickened. Remove from the heat and pour it over the vegetables.

4. Leave to cool, then cover and chill in the refrigerator for at least 2 hours before serving.

Serves 4

- 25 g/1 oz butter
- 2 tbsp olive oil
- 1 onion, finely chopped
- 2 garlic cloves, finely chopped
- 1 celery stick, finely chopped
- 500 g/1 lb 2 oz plum tomatoes, peeled, cored and chopped
- 2 tbsp tomato purée
- brown sugar, to taste
- 150 ml/5 fl oz dry white wine
- 1 tbsp lemon juice
- 1 tbsp chopped fresh parsley
- 8 shallots, trimmed and peeled
- 225 g/8 oz cauliflower florets
- 8 button mushrooms
- salt and pepper

Baked Aubergine with Tomato Sauce & Parmesan

1. First, make the sauce. Melt the butter with the oil in a saucepan. Add the onion, garlic and celery and cook over a low heat, stirring occasionally, for 5 minutes, until softened. Stir in the tomatoes, tomato purée, sugar to taste, basil, oregano and water and season to taste with salt and pepper. Increase the heat to medium and bring to the boil, then reduce the heat and simmer, stirring occasionally, for 15–20 minutes, until thickened.

2. Preheat the oven to 230°C/450°F/Gas Mark 8. Grease a baking sheet with butter. Melt the butter and pour it into a shallow dish. Spread out the breadcrumbs in a separate shallow dish. Dip the aubergine slices first in the melted butter and then in the breadcrumbs to coat. Put them on the prepared baking sheet and season to taste with salt. Bake in the preheated oven for 20 minutes, until golden brown and tender.

3. Remove the baking sheet from the oven. Top each aubergine slice with a spoonful of tomato sauce and sprinkle with a little of the oregano and Parmesan. Return to the oven and bake for a further 10 minutes, until the topping is golden brown. Transfer to a serving dish, garnish with basil and serve immediately.

Serves 6

40 g/1½ oz butter, plus extra for greasing

40 g/1½ oz dry breadcrumbs

1 large aubergine, cut into 1-cm/½-inch slices

1 tsp dried oregano

55 g/2 oz Parmesan cheese, grated

salt

Tomato sauce
* 25 g/1 oz butter
* 2 tbsp olive oil
* 1 small onion, finely chopped
* 1 garlic clove, finely chopped
* 1 celery stick, finely chopped
* 400 g/14 oz canned chopped tomatoes
* 2 tbsp tomato purée
* brown sugar, to taste
* 1 tbsp chopped fresh basil, plus extra to garnish
* 1 tsp dried oregano
* 100 ml/3½ fl oz water
* salt and pepper

Fettuccine with Tomato & Mushroom Sauce

1. First, make the sauce. Melt the butter with the oil in a saucepan. Add the onion, garlic and celery and cook over a low heat, stirring occasionally, for 5 minutes, until softened. Stir in the tomatoes, tomato purée, wine and mushrooms. Increase the heat to medium and bring to the boil, then reduce the heat and simmer, stirring occasionally, for 15–20 minutes, until thickened.

2. Meanwhile, bring a large saucepan of lightly salted water to the boil. Add the fettuccine, bring back to the boil and cook for 8–10 minutes, until tender but still firm to the bite. Drain, tip into a warmed serving dish and toss with the butter.

3. Stir sugar to taste and the basil into the sauce and season to taste with salt and pepper. Pour the sauce over the pasta, toss well and sprinkle with the Parmesan. Serve immediately.

Serves 4

450 g/1 lb dried fettuccine
15 g/½ oz butter
2 tbsp grated Parmesan cheese
salt

Tomato & mushroom sauce
* 25 g/1 oz butter
* 2 tbsp olive oil
* 1 large onion, finely chopped
* 2 garlic cloves, finely chopped
* 1 celery stick, finely chopped
* 400 g/14 oz canned chopped tomatoes
* 2 tbsp tomato purée
  4 tbsp dry red wine
  115 g/4 oz mushrooms, sliced
* brown sugar, to taste
* 1 tbsp chopped fresh basil
* salt and pepper

Tomato Soufflé

1 First, make the sauce. Melt the butter with the oil in a saucepan. Add the onion, garlic and celery and cook over a low heat, stirring occasionally, for 5 minutes, until softened. Stir in the canned tomatoes, tomato purée, sugar to taste, ginger, bay leaf and water and season to taste with salt and pepper. Increase the heat to medium and bring to the boil, then reduce the heat and simmer, stirring occasionally, for 15–20 minutes, until thickened.

2 Meanwhile, cook the potatoes in a large saucepan of salted boiling water for 20–25 minutes, until tender but not falling apart. Drain well and set aside.

3 Preheat the oven to 230°C/450°F/Gas Mark 8. Brush a 1.5-litre/2¾-pint soufflé dish with oil and dust with flour, tipping out the excess. Remove the sauce from the heat and leave to cool slightly. Remove and discard the bay leaf. Pour the sauce into a food processor, add the potatoes and process to a purée. Transfer to a bowl and stir in the diced tomato, egg yolk and oil. Taste and adjust the seasoning, adding salt and pepper if needed.

4 Whisk the egg whites in a grease-free bowl until they form soft peaks. Stir one quarter of the egg whites into the tomato mixture, then fold in the remainder. Pour into the prepared dish and bake in the preheated oven for 35–40 minutes, until risen and golden brown. Serve immediately.

Serves 4

350 g/12 oz potatoes, cut into chunks

plain flour, for dusting

1 beef tomato, peeled, deseeded and diced

1 egg, separated

1 tbsp olive oil, plus extra for brushing

4 egg whites

salt and pepper

Tomato sauce

25 g/1 oz butter

2 tbsp olive oil

1 onion, finely chopped

2 garlic cloves, finely chopped

1 celery stick, finely chopped

400 g/14 oz canned chopped tomatoes

2 tbsp tomato purée

brown sugar, to taste

1 tsp chopped fresh ginger

1 bay leaf

100 ml/3½ fl oz water

salt and pepper

Special Macaroni Cheese

1. First, make the sauce. Melt the butter with the oil in a saucepan. Add the onion, garlic and celery and cook over a low heat, stirring occasionally, for 5 minutes, until softened. Stir in the tomatoes, tomato purée, sugar to taste, basil and water and season to taste with salt and pepper. Increase the heat to medium and bring to the boil, then reduce the heat and simmer, stirring occasionally, for 15–20 minutes, until thickened.

2. Meanwhile, preheat the oven to 190°C/375°F/Gas Mark 5. Grease an ovenproof dish with butter. Bring a large saucepan of lightly salted water to the boil. Add the macaroni, bring back to the boil and cook for 8–10 minutes, until tender but still firm to the bite. Drain well.

3. Mix together the Parmesan and Gruyère in a bowl. Spoon one third of the tomato sauce into the prepared dish, cover with one third of the macaroni and sprinkle with one third of the mixed cheeses. Repeat twice. Mix together the breadcrumbs and the basil and sprinkle over the top. Dot with the butter and bake in the preheated oven for 20–25 minutes, until the topping is golden brown. Serve immediately.

Serves 4

225 g/8 oz dried macaroni

115 g/4 oz Parmesan cheese, grated

175 g/6 oz Gruyère cheese, grated

25 g/1 oz fresh breadcrumbs

1 tbsp chopped fresh basil

15 g/½ oz butter, plus extra for greasing

salt

Tomato sauce

* 25 g/1 oz butter
* 2 tbsp olive oil
* 1 small onion, finely chopped
* 2 garlic cloves, finely chopped
* 1 celery stick, finely chopped
* 400 g/14 oz canned chopped tomatoes
* 2 tbsp tomato purée
* brown sugar, to taste
* 1 tbsp chopped fresh basil
* 100 ml/3½ fl oz water
* salt and pepper

Spicy

Beef Enchiladas in Piquant Tomato Sauce

1. Heat the corn oil in a frying pan. Add the onion and chillies and cook over a low heat, stirring occasionally, for 5 minutes. Add the beef, increase the heat to medium and cook, stirring frequently and breaking it up with the spoon, for 8–10 minutes, until evenly browned. Remove the pan from the heat and stir in half the cheese.

2. To make the sauce, melt the butter with the olive oil in a saucepan. Add the onion, garlic and chilli and cook over a medium heat, stirring occasionally, for 5–8 minutes, until the onion is golden brown. Stir in the tomatoes, tomato purée, sugar to taste, oregano and cayenne pepper and season to taste with salt and pepper. Increase the heat to medium and bring to the boil. Reduce the heat, stir in the cream and simmer, stirring occasionally, for 15–20 minutes, until thickened. Remove from the heat and leave to cool slightly.

3. Meanwhile, preheat the oven to 180°C/350°F/Gas Mark 4. Heat a frying pan and brush with corn oil. One at a time, dip the tortillas in the sauce, shake off any excess and cook in the frying pan for 30 seconds on each side. Transfer to a large plate, put a tablespoon of the meat mixture in the centre and roll up. Put the filled tortillas, seam-side down, in a large ovenproof dish and pour the remaining sauce over them. Sprinkle with the remaining cheese and bake in the preheated oven for 15–20 minutes. Garnish with coriander and serve immediately.

Serves 6

- 1 tbsp corn oil, plus extra for brushing
- 1 onion, finely chopped
- 2 fresh green chillies, deseeded and chopped
- 280 g/10 oz fresh beef mince
- 115 g/4 oz Cheddar cheese, grated
- 18 tortillas
- chopped fresh coriander, to garnish

Piquant tomato sauce
- 25 g/1 oz butter
- 2 tbsp olive oil
- 1 onion, finely chopped
- 2 garlic cloves, finely chopped
- 1 fresh green chilli, deseeded and chopped
- 400 g/14 oz canned chopped tomatoes
- 2 tbsp tomato purée
- brown sugar, to taste
- 1 tsp dried oregano
- ½ tsp cayenne pepper
- 125 ml/4 fl oz double cream
- salt and pepper

46

Spicy Meatballs

1. First, make the meatballs. Mix together the pork, grated onion, garlic, breadcrumbs, almonds, egg, cinnamon and sherry, kneading with your hands until thoroughly combined. Shape the mixture into 36 walnut-sized balls.

2. Heat the oil in a frying pan. Add the meatballs, in batches, and cook over a medium heat, turning frequently, for 6–8 minutes, until evenly browned. Remove with a slotted spoon, set aside and keep warm.

3. Add the chopped onion, the garlic and sugar to the frying pan and cook over a low heat, stirring occasionally, for 8–10 minutes, until the onion is golden brown. Add the tomatoes, peppers, chillies, tomato purée, coriander and paprika and cook, stirring occasionally, for a further 5 minutes. Pour in 150 ml/5 fl oz of the stock, season to taste with salt and pepper, increase the heat and bring to the boil.

4. Meanwhile, mix the cornflour to a paste with the remaining stock in a bowl. Reduce the heat, stir in the cornflour mixture and add the meatballs. Cover and simmer for 20–25 minutes, until the meatballs are cooked through. Transfer to a warmed serving dish, garnish with coriander and serve immediately.

Serves 6

- 3 tbsp corn oil
- 1 large onion, finely chopped
- 1 garlic clove, finely chopped
- 1 tbsp brown sugar
- 400 g/14 oz canned chopped tomatoes
- 1 red and 1 green pepper, deseeded and sliced
- 2 fresh green chillies, chopped
- 2 tbsp tomato purée
- 1 tbsp chopped fresh coriander, plus extra to garnish
- 1 tsp paprika
- 200 ml/7 fl oz chicken stock
- 2 tsp cornflour
- salt and pepper

Meatballs
- 1 kg/2 lb 4 oz fresh pork mince
- 1 large onion, grated
- 2 garlic cloves, finely chopped
- 55 g/2 oz fresh breadcrumbs
- 55 g/2 oz ground almonds
- 1 egg, lightly beaten
- 1 tsp ground cinnamon
- 3 tbsp dry sherry

109

47

Pork Chops Mexican Style

1. Rub the pork chops all over with the cut sides of the garlic. Put them on a plate, cover with clingfilm and chill in the refrigerator for 4 hours.

2. Meanwhile, make the sauce. Melt the butter with the olive oil in a saucepan. Add the onion, garlic and celery and cook over a low heat, stirring occasionally, for 5 minutes, until softened. Stir in the tomatoes, tomato purée, sugar to taste, chillies and water and season to taste with salt and pepper. Increase the heat to medium and bring to the boil, then reduce the heat and simmer, stirring occasionally, for 20 minutes. Remove from the heat and leave to cool slightly, then transfer to a food processor or blender and process to a purée.

3. Heat the corn oil in a large frying pan. Add the pork chops and cook over a medium heat for 5 minutes on each side, until evenly browned. Pour in the sauce, reduce the heat, cover and simmer, turning the chops once or twice, for 15–20 minutes, until cooked through and tender.

4. Meanwhile, peel, stone and slice the avocado, then sprinkle with the lime juice to prevent discoloration. When the chops are ready, transfer to a warmed serving dish, pour the sauce over them and top with the avocado. Serve immediately.

Serves 4

4 pork chops
2 garlic cloves, halved
2 tbsp corn oil
1 avocado
2 tbsp lime juice

Tomato & chilli sauce
25 g/1 oz butter
2 tbsp olive oil
1 onion, finely chopped
2 garlic cloves, finely chopped
1 celery stick, finely chopped
650 g/1 lb 7 oz plum tomatoes, peeled, cored and chopped
2 tbsp tomato purée
brown sugar, to taste
3 fresh green chillies, finely chopped
300 ml/10 fl oz water
salt and pepper

48

Loin of Pork with Spicy Tomato Sauce

1. First, make the sauce. Melt the butter with the olive oil in a saucepan. Add the onion, garlic and celery and cook over a low heat, stirring occasionally, for 5 minutes, until softened. Stir in the tomatoes, tomato purée, soy sauce, chilli sauce, Worcestershire sauce, vinegar, mustard, sugar to taste and bay leaf. Increase the heat to medium and bring to the boil, then reduce the heat and simmer, stirring occasionally, for 15–20 minutes, until thickened.

2. Meanwhile, preheat the oven to 180°C/350°F/Gas Mark 4. Mix together the sugar, ginger and cayenne in a small bowl and stir in a pinch of each salt and pepper. Rub the mixture all over the pork.

3. Heat the sunflower oil in a large flameproof casserole. Add the pork and cook over a medium heat, turning frequently, until evenly browned. Drain off the oil. Pour the sauce over the pork, cover the casserole and transfer to the preheated oven. Cook, occasionally spooning the sauce over the meat, for 1¾ hours.

4. Remove the meat from the casserole, cover with foil and leave to rest. Meanwhile, bring the sauce to the boil over a medium heat. Skim off any fat. Cut the pork into slices, put them on a warmed serving dish and strain the sauce over them, pressing down with the back of a spoon. Garnish with sage and serve immediately.

Serves 6

1 tbsp brown sugar

½ tsp ground ginger

½ tsp cayenne pepper

1.8 kg/4 lb boned and rolled loin of pork

2 tbsp sunflower oil

salt and pepper

chopped fresh sage, to garnish

Spicy tomato sauce

* 25 g/1 oz butter
* 2 tbsp olive oil
* 1 onion, finely chopped
* 2 garlic cloves, finely chopped
* 1 celery stick, finely chopped
* 400 g/14 oz canned chopped tomatoes
* 2 tbsp tomato purée

2 tbsp light soy sauce

2 tbsp chilli sauce

2 tbsp Worcestershire sauce

1 tbsp white wine vinegar

2 tsp Dijon mustard

* brown sugar, to taste
* 1 bay leaf

51

Chicken with Tomato & Cinnamon Sauce

1. Melt the butter with the oil in a flameproof casserole. Season the chicken well with salt and pepper, add to the casserole and cook over a medium heat, turning frequently, for 8–10 minutes, until evenly browned. Remove from the casserole and set aside.

2. Add the onion, garlic and celery to the casserole and cook over a low heat, stirring occasionally, for 5 minutes, until softened. Stir in the tomatoes, tomato purée, mustard, sugar to taste, lemon juice, stock, oregano and cinnamon and season to taste with salt and pepper. Increase the heat to medium and bring to the boil, then reduce the heat and simmer, stirring occasionally, for 15 minutes.

3. Return the chicken to the casserole and spoon the sauce over it. Cover and simmer, stirring occasionally, for 30 minutes, until the chicken is tender and cooked through. Serve immediately.

Serves 4

* 55 g/2 oz butter
* 2 tbsp olive oil
  4 chicken quarters
* 1 onion, finely chopped
* 2 garlic cloves, finely chopped
* 1 celery stick, finely chopped
* 400 g/14 oz canned chopped tomatoes
* 2 tbsp tomato purée
  1 tsp Dijon mustard
* brown sugar, to taste
  2 tbsp lemon juice
  3 tbsp chicken stock
* 1 tsp dried oregano
  ¾ tsp ground cinnamon
* salt and pepper

Devilled Chicken

1. Put the chicken, carrots, celery, peppercorns, bouquet garni and salt into a large saucepan and pour in water to cover. Bring to the boil over a high heat, then reduce the heat, cover and simmer for 1½ hours, until tender and cooked through. Remove from the heat and leave to cool.

2. Meanwhile, make the sauce. Melt the butter with the oil in a saucepan. Add the shallots, garlic and celery and cook over a low heat, stirring occasionally, for 5 minutes, until softened. Stir in the tomatoes, tomato purée, sugar to taste, Worcestershire sauce, lemon juice, vinegar and bay leaf and season to taste with salt and pepper. Increase the heat to medium and bring to the boil, then reduce the heat and simmer, stirring occasionally, for 15–20 minutes, until thickened.

3. Preheat the grill. Remove the chicken from the pan and strain the cooking liquid into a bowl. Remove and discard the skin, cut the chicken into eight pieces and put them into a flameproof casserole. Brush the chicken with the melted butter and cook under the preheated grill for 8 minutes on each side, until evenly browned.

4. Remove and discard the bay leaf from the sauce and stir in 300 ml/10 fl oz of the reserved cooking liquid. Pour the sauce over the chicken and cook over a medium heat for 10–15 minutes, until the chicken is cooked through. Garnish with thyme and serve immediately.

Serves 4

1 whole chicken, weighing 2.25 kg/5 lb
2 carrots, cut into chunks
1 celery stick, cut into lengths
6 black peppercorns
1 bouquet garni
pinch of salt
25 g/1 oz butter, melted
fresh thyme leaves, to garnish

Devil sauce
* 25 g/1 oz butter
* 2 tbsp olive oil
2 shallots, finely chopped
* 2 garlic cloves, finely chopped
* 1 celery stick, finely chopped
* 400 g/14 oz canned chopped tomatoes
* 2 tbsp tomato purée
* brown sugar, to taste
3 tbsp Worcestershire sauce
1 tbsp lemon juice
2 tbsp tarragon vinegar
* 1 bay leaf
* salt and pepper

Cajun Chicken

1. Heat the oil in a flameproof casserole. Add the chicken and cook over a medium heat, for 3–5 minutes on each side, until evenly browned. Remove and set aside.

2. Reduce the heat to low, stir in half the flour and cook, stirring constantly, for 1 minute, then stir in the remaining flour. Cook, stirring constantly, until the mixture is the colour of peanut butter. Immediately add the onion, garlic, celery and green pepper and cook, stirring constantly, for 4 minutes. Add the oregano, thyme, bay leaf and chillies and cook, stirring, for a further minute, then remove the casserole from the heat and stir in the tomatoes, tomato purée and sugar to taste. Season to taste with salt and pepper.

3. Return the casserole to the heat and gradually stir in the stock. Bring to the boil, stirring constantly, then return the chicken to the casserole. Reduce the heat, cover and simmer, stirring occasionally, for 45 minutes, until the chicken is tender and cooked through. If the sauce seems too runny, remove the lid for the final 15 minutes of the cooking time. Remove and discard the bay leaf.

4. Taste and adjust the seasoning, adding salt and pepper if needed, and stir in the Tabasco, if using. Serve immediately.

Serves 4

- 5 tbsp olive oil
- 4 chicken breasts, about 175 g/6 oz each
- 55 g/2 oz plain flour
- 1 onion, finely chopped
- 2 garlic cloves, finely chopped
- 1 celery stick, finely chopped
- 1 green pepper, deseeded and chopped
- ½ tsp dried oregano
- ½ tsp dried thyme
- 1 bay leaf
- 2 fresh red chillies, deseeded and chopped
- 400 g/14 oz canned chopped tomatoes
- 2 tbsp tomato purée
- brown sugar, to taste
- 300 ml/10 fl oz chicken stock
- dash of Tabasco sauce (optional)
- salt and pepper

54

Chicken & Spicy Tomato Sauce Parcels

1. First, make the sauce. Melt the butter with the oil in a saucepan. Add the onion, garlic, celery and peppers and cook over a low heat, stirring occasionally, for 5 minutes, until softened. Stir in the tomatoes, sun-dried tomato paste, sugar to taste, paprika, chilli powder, thyme and water and season to taste with salt and pepper. Increase the heat to medium and bring to the boil, then reduce the heat and simmer, stirring occasionally, for 15–20 minutes, until thickened.

2. Meanwhile, preheat the oven to 190°C/375°F/Gas Mark 5. Cut four squares of greaseproof paper, each large enough to enclose a chicken breast. Put one chicken breast on each square.

3. Divide the sauce among the chicken fillets and top each with a tarragon sprig. Fold the paper over fairly loosely and double-fold the edges to seal. Put the parcels on a baking sheet and bake in the preheated oven for 35–40 minutes, until the chicken is cooked through and tender. Serve immediately.

Serves 4

4 chicken breasts, about 175 g/6 oz each

4 fresh tarragon sprigs

Spicy tomato sauce
* 25 g/1 oz butter
* 2 tbsp olive oil
* 1 onion, finely chopped
* 2 garlic cloves, finely chopped
* 1 celery stick, finely chopped
* 2 orange peppers, deseeded and chopped
* 400 g/14 oz canned chopped tomatoes
* 2 tbsp sun-dried tomato paste
* brown sugar, to taste
* 1 tbsp paprika
* 1 tsp chilli powder
* 1 tsp dried thyme
* 100 ml/3½ fl oz water
* salt and pepper

55

Red Snapper in Hot Pepper & Tomato Sauce

1. First, make the sauce. Heat the oil in a saucepan, then add the onion, garlic, celery and chilli and cook over a low heat, stirring occasionally, for 5 minutes, until softened. Stir in the pimientos, tomatoes, tomato purée, sugar to taste, coriander, olives and water and season to taste with salt and pepper. Increase the heat to medium and bring to the boil, then reduce the heat and simmer, stirring occasionally, for 15–20 minutes, until thickened.

2. Meanwhile, preheat the oven to 180°C/350°F/Gas Mark 4. Mix together the flour, chilli powder, salt and pepper in a plastic bag. Add the fish fillets, a few at a time, hold the top closed and shake gently to coat. Heat the oil in a frying pan, then add the fish, in batches, and cook for 5 minutes on each side, until golden brown. Transfer the fish to a large ovenproof dish and set aside.

3. Halve the eggs, remove the yolks and chop. (You do not need the whites.)

4. Pour the sauce over the fish and bake in the preheated oven for 10–15 minutes, until the flesh flakes easily. Sprinkle with the chopped egg yolks. Garnish with coriander and serve immediately.

Serves 4

55 g/2 oz plain flour·
1 tsp chilli powder
1 tsp salt
1 tsp pepper
900 g/2 lb red snapper fillets
3 tbsp olive oil
2 hard-boiled eggs

Hot pepper & tomato sauce
* 2 tbsp olive oil
* 1 onion, finely chopped
* 2 garlic cloves, finely chopped
* 1 celery stick, finely chopped
* 1 fresh red chilli, finely chopped
* 115 g/4 oz drained pimientos, finely chopped
* 400 g/14 oz canned chopped tomatoes
* 2 tbsp tomato purée
* brown sugar, to taste
* 1 tbsp chopped fresh coriander, plus extra to garnish
* 55 g/2 oz pimiento-stuffed olives, sliced
* 100 ml/3½ fl oz water
* salt and pepper

56

Fish with Indian Tomato Sauce

1. Mix together 1 teaspoon of salt and 1½ teaspoons of the turmeric in a small bowl. Gently rub the mixture all over the fish cubes. Heat the oil in a deep frying pan. Add the fish cubes and cook over a medium heat, turning frequently, for 5 minutes, until golden brown. Remove with a slotted spoon and set aside.

2. Reduce the heat, add the onions and cook, stirring occasionally, for 8–10 minutes, until golden brown. Stir in the garlic, sugar, ground coriander, chilli flakes, garam masala and the remaining turmeric and cook, stirring constantly, for 2 minutes. Add the tomatoes, tomato purée, soured cream, lime juice and chillies, increase the heat and bring to the boil. Reduce the heat and simmer, stirring occasionally, for 15 minutes, until thickened.

3. Return the fish cubes to the pan and simmer, stirring occasionally, for 10 minutes. Taste and adjust the seasoning, adding salt and pepper if needed. Transfer to a warmed serving dish and serve immediately.

Serves 4

- 2 tsp ground turmeric
- 1 kg/2 lb 4 oz monkfish fillet, cut into 4-cm/1½-inch cubes
- 4 tbsp groundnut oil
- 2 onions, thinly sliced
- 2 garlic cloves, finely chopped
- 1 tsp brown sugar
- 1 tbsp ground coriander
- 1 tsp chilli flakes
- 2 tsp garam masala
- 500 g/1 lb 2 oz plum tomatoes, peeled, cored and finely chopped
- 2 tbsp tomato purée
- 2 tbsp soured cream
- 1 tbsp lime juice
- 4 fresh green chillies, slit in half lengthways and deseeded
- salt and pepper

61

Courgette Fritters with Peppery Tomato Sauce

1. First, make the sauce. Melt the butter with the oil in a saucepan. Add the shallots, garlic, celery and cloves and cook over a low heat, stirring occasionally, for 5 minutes, until softened. Remove and discard the garlic and cloves. Add the breadcrumbs and cook, stirring frequently, for 3 minutes. Stir in the tomatoes, tomato purée, sugar to taste and water. Increase the heat to medium and bring to the boil, then reduce the heat and simmer, stirring occasionally, for 30 minutes, until thickened.

2. Meanwhile, coarsely grate the courgettes onto a clean tea towel, then gather up the sides and squeeze tightly to remove the excess moisture. Transfer the courgettes to a bowl, stir in the cheese, eggs and flour and season to taste with salt and pepper.

3. Pour the groundnut oil into a large frying pan to a depth of 2 cm/¾ inch and heat. Add three heaps of the courgette mixture, each 2 tablespoonfuls, flatten slightly and cook for 2–3 minutes on each side. Remove and drain on kitchen paper. Keep warm while you cook more fritters in the same way until all the mixture has been used.

4. Transfer the fritters to a warmed serving plate. Remove the sauce from the heat and season lightly with salt and very generously with pepper and transfer to a warmed serving bowl. Serve immediately.

Serves 4–6

500 g/1 lb 2 oz courgettes

55 g/2 oz Parmesan cheese, grated

2 eggs, lightly beaten

4 tbsp plain flour

groundnut oil, for deep-frying

salt and pepper

Peppery tomato sauce

✳ 25 g/1 oz butter

✳ 2 tbsp olive oil

2 shallots, finely chopped

✳ 2 garlic cloves

✳ 1 celery stick, finely chopped

2 cloves

3 tbsp dry breadcrumbs

✳ 400 g/14 oz canned chopped tomatoes

✳ 2 tbsp tomato purée

✳ brown sugar, to taste

✳ 100 ml/3½ fl oz water

✳ salt and pepper

Comforting

62

Little Spanish Meatballs in Smooth Tomato Sauce

1. First, make the sauce. Melt the butter with the oil in a large flameproof casserole. Add the shallots, garlic and celery and cook over a low heat, stirring occasionally, for 5 minutes, until softened. Stir in the tomatoes, tomato purée, sugar, thyme, bay leaf and milk and season to taste with salt and pepper. Increase the heat to medium and bring to the boil, then reduce the heat and simmer, stirring frequently, for 30 minutes, until thickened.

2. Meanwhile, using your hands, mix together the beef, onion, red pepper, rice, paprika and egg in a large bowl until thoroughly combined. Dust your hands with flour and shape pieces of the mixture into balls about 4 cm/1½ inches in diameter. Set aside.

3. Remove the casserole from the heat. Remove and discard the bay leaf, then strain the sauce into a bowl, pressing the vegetables through with the back of a wooden spoon. Return the sauce to the casserole and stir in the cayenne pepper.

4. Add the meatballs to the casserole and bring to the boil over a medium heat. Reduce the heat, cover and simmer for 40–45 minutes, until the meatballs are cooked through. Serve immediately.

Serves 6

700 g/1 lb 9 oz fresh beef mince

1 onion, finely chopped

1 red pepper, deseeded and chopped

85 g/3 oz long-grain rice, soaked for 30 minutes and drained

1 tbsp paprika

1 large egg, lightly beaten

plain flour, for dusting

Smooth tomato sauce

25 g/1 oz butter

2 tbsp olive oil

2 shallots, finely chopped

2 garlic cloves, finely chopped

1 celery stick, finely chopped

400 g/14 oz canned chopped tomatoes

4 tbsp tomato purée

1 tbsp brown sugar

1 tbsp chopped fresh thyme

1 bay leaf

225 ml/8 fl oz milk

pinch of cayenne pepper

salt and pepper

Cabbage Rolls with Beef in Sweet Tomato Sauce

1. Bring a large saucepan of water to the boil, add the whole cabbage and boil for 4 minutes. Drain and leave to cool slightly, then separate the leaves.

2. Using your hands, mix together the beef, fresh tomatoes, rice, lemon juice and rind and parsley in a bowl and season to taste with salt and pepper. Shape the mixture into about 12 small sausage shapes. Wrap each in a cabbage leaf, tucking in the sides, and tie with fine string. Set aside.

3. To make the sauce, melt the butter with the olive oil in a saucepan. Add the onion, garlic and celery and cook over a low heat, stirring occasionally, for 5 minutes, until softened. Stir in the canned tomatoes, tomato purée, sugar, honey, basil and water and season to taste with salt and pepper. Increase the heat to medium and bring to the boil, then reduce the heat and simmer, stirring occasionally, for 15–20 minutes, until thickened.

4. Heat the sunflower oil in a large saucepan. Add the cabbage rolls and cook over a medium heat, turning frequently, for a few minutes, until lightly browned. Reduce the heat and pour the sauce over them, then cover and simmer for 1 hour.

5. Using a slotted spoon, remove the rolls from the pan. Remove and discard the string and transfer the rolls to a serving dish. Serve immediately with the sauce.

Serves 4

1 head of Savoy cabbage, coarse leaves removed

500 g/1 lb 2 oz fresh beef mince

2 tomatoes, peeled and chopped

2 tbsp long-grain rice

juice and grated rind of ½ lemon

1 tbsp chopped fresh parsley

3 tbsp sunflower oil

salt and pepper

Sweet tomato sauce

* 25 g/1 oz butter
* 2 tbsp olive oil
* 1 onion, finely chopped
* 2 garlic cloves, finely chopped
* 1 celery stick, finely chopped
* 400 g/14 oz canned chopped tomatoes
* 2 tbsp tomato purée
* 1 tbsp brown sugar
  1 tbsp clear honey
* 1 tbsp chopped fresh basil
* 100 ml/3½ fl oz water
* salt and pepper

Pork Chops with Tomato & Mushroom Sauce

1. Preheat the grill to high. Brush the chops with the sunflower oil, sprinkle with the sage and season well with salt and pepper. Cook under the preheated grill for 5 minutes on each side, then reduce the heat and grill for a further 10–15 minutes on each side, until cooked through and tender.

2. Meanwhile, make the sauce. Melt the butter with the olive oil in a saucepan. Add the shallots, garlic and celery and cook over a low heat, stirring occasionally, for 5 minutes, until softened. Add the mushrooms and cook, stirring occasionally, for a further 3 minutes. Stir in the tomatoes, tomato purée, sugar to taste, parsley and water and season to taste with salt and pepper. Increase the heat to medium and bring to the boil, then reduce the heat and simmer, stirring occasionally, for 15–20 minutes, until thickened.

3. Transfer the chops to warmed serving plates. Pour the sauce over them and serve immediately.

Serves 4

4 boneless pork chops
2 tbsp sunflower oil
1 tsp dried sage
salt and pepper

Tomato & mushroom sauce
25 g/1 oz butter
2 tbsp olive oil
2 shallots, finely chopped
2 garlic cloves, finely chopped
1 celery stick, finely chopped
115 g/4 oz mushrooms, sliced
400 g/14 oz canned chopped tomatoes
2 tbsp tomato purée
brown sugar, to taste
2 tbsp chopped fresh flat-leaf parsley
100 ml/3½ fl oz water
salt and pepper

One-pot Lamb in Rich Red Sauce

1. Cook the lamb cutlets in a large frying pan without any added fat over a medium heat for 2–3 minutes on each side, until lightly browned. Remove the pan from the heat and transfer the cutlets to a plate.

2. Wipe out the pan with kitchen paper and return to the heat. Melt the butter with the oil in the pan. Add the onion, garlic, celery and peppers and cook over a low heat, stirring occasionally, for 5 minutes, until softened. Stir in the tomatoes, tomato purée, sugar to taste, basil and water and season to taste with salt and pepper. Increase the heat to medium and bring to the boil.

3. Return the cutlets to the pan, spooning the sauce over them. Reduce the heat and simmer, stirring occasionally, for 15–20 minutes, until the sauce has thickened and the lamb is tender. Stir in the olives, then taste and adjust the seasoning, adding salt and pepper if needed. Garnish with basil and serve immediately.

Serves 4

12 lamb cutlets, trimmed of excess fat
* 25 g/1 oz butter
* 2 tbsp olive oil
* 1 onion, finely chopped
* 2 garlic cloves, finely chopped
* 1 celery stick, finely chopped
  2 red peppers, deseeded and sliced
* 400 g/14 oz canned chopped tomatoes
* 2 tbsp tomato purée
* brown sugar, to taste
* 2 tbsp chopped fresh basil, plus extra to garnish
* 100 ml/3½ fl oz water
  2 tbsp chopped stoned black olives
* salt and pepper

Lamb Hash with Mushrooms & Tomato Sauce

1. First, make the sauce. Melt the butter with the oil in a saucepan. Add the onion, garlic and celery and cook over a low heat, stirring occasionally, for 5 minutes, until softened. Stir in the tomatoes, tomato purée, sugar to taste, basil, oregano and water and season to taste with salt and pepper. Increase the heat to medium and bring to the boil, then reduce the heat and simmer, stirring occasionally, for 15–20 minutes, until thickened.

2. Preheat the oven to 180°C/350°F/Gas Mark 4. Meanwhile, chop the mushrooms. Melt half the butter in a large saucepan, add the mushrooms and cook over a medium heat, stirring frequently, for 5 minutes, until softened. Stir in the flour and cook, stirring constantly, for 1 minute, then remove the pan from the heat. Gradually stir in the stock, a little at a time, then return the pan to the heat and cook, stirring constantly, for 3–4 minutes, until thick and smooth. Remove the pan from the heat and stir in the sherry, parsley and lamb. Transfer to a large ovenproof dish and set aside.

3. Pour the sauce over the lamb mixture. Mix together the cheese and breadcrumbs in a small bowl and sprinkle over the top. Dot with the remaining butter and bake in the preheated oven for 30 minutes, until the topping is golden and crisp. Serve immediately.

Serves 4

225 g/8 oz mushrooms
50 g/1¾ oz butter
1 tbsp plain flour
300 ml/10 fl oz chicken stock
1 tbsp dry sherry
1 tbsp chopped fresh parsley
500 g/1 lb 2 oz boneless cooked lamb, chopped
55 g/2 oz Cheddar cheese, grated
25 g/1 oz fresh breadcrumbs

Tomato sauce
25 g/1 oz butter
2 tbsp olive oil
1 onion, finely chopped
2 garlic cloves, finely chopped
1 celery stick, finely chopped
400 g/14 oz canned chopped tomatoes
2 tbsp tomato purée
brown sugar, to taste
1 tbsp chopped fresh basil
1 tsp dried oregano
100 ml/3½ fl oz water
salt and pepper

Fried Chicken with Tomato & Bacon Sauce

1 First, make the sauce. Melt the butter with the oil in a large saucepan. Add the onion, garlic, celery and bacon and cook over a low heat, stirring occasionally, for 5 minutes, until softened. Stir in the tomatoes, tomato purée, sugar to taste and water and season to taste with salt and pepper. Increase the heat to medium and bring to the boil, then reduce the heat and simmer, stirring occasionally, for 15–20 minutes, until thickened.

2 Meanwhile, melt the butter with the oil in a large frying pan. Add the chicken and cook over a medium–high heat for 4–5 minutes on each side, until evenly browned.

3 Stir the basil and parsley into the sauce. Add the chicken and spoon the sauce over it. Cover and simmer for 10–15 minutes, until cooked through and tender. Garnish with parsley and serve immediately.

Serves 4

25 g/1 oz butter

2 tbsp olive oil

4 skinless, boneless chicken breasts or 8 skinless, boneless chicken thighs

Tomato & bacon sauce

* 25 g/1 oz butter
* 2 tbsp olive oil
* 1 large onion, finely chopped
* 2 garlic cloves, finely chopped
* 1 celery stick, finely chopped
  4 rashers bacon, diced
* 400 g/14 oz canned chopped tomatoes
* 2 tbsp tomato purée
* brown sugar, to taste
* 100 ml/3½ fl oz water
* 1 tbsp chopped fresh basil
* 1 tbsp chopped fresh parsley, plus extra to garnish
* salt and pepper

Chicken with Tomato Sauce & Melted Mozzarella

1. First, make the sauce. Melt the butter with the oil in a saucepan. Add the onion, garlic and celery and cook over a low heat, stirring occasionally, for 5 minutes, until softened. Stir in the tomatoes, tomato purée, sugar to taste, oregano and water and season to taste with salt and pepper. Increase the heat to medium and bring to the boil, then reduce the heat and simmer, stirring occasionally, for 15–20 minutes, until thickened.

2. Meanwhile, fry the bacon without any additional fat in a large frying pan over a medium heat for 5 minutes. Remove with tongs and drain on kitchen paper. Add the butter to the pan and, when it has melted, stir in the tarragon, add the chicken and cook, turning occasionally, for 15–20 minutes, until cooked through and tender.

3. Preheat the grill. Transfer the chicken to an ovenproof dish and put a bacon rasher on top of each fillet. Pour the sauce over them, cover with the mozzarella slices and cook under the preheated grill for 4–5 minutes, until the cheese has melted and is lightly browned. Serve immediately.

Serves 6

6 rashers bacon

25 g/1 oz butter

2 tsp chopped fresh tarragon

6 skinless, boneless chicken breasts, about 175 g/ 6 oz each

115 g/4 oz mozzarella cheese, sliced

Tomato sauce

25 g/1 oz butter

2 tbsp olive oil

1 onion, finely chopped

2 garlic cloves, finely chopped

1 celery stick, finely chopped

400 g/14 oz canned chopped tomatoes

2 tbsp tomato purée

brown sugar, to taste

1 tsp dried oregano

100 ml/3½ fl oz water

salt and pepper

72

Salmon & Potatoes with Tomato Sauce Topping

1. First, make the sauce. Melt the butter with the oil in a saucepan. Add the onions, garlic and celery and cook over a low heat, stirring occasionally, for 5 minutes, until softened. Stir in the tomatoes, tomato purée, sugar to taste, marjoram and wine and season to taste with salt and pepper. Increase the heat to medium and bring to the boil, then reduce the heat and simmer, stirring occasionally, for 15–20 minutes, until thickened.

2. Meanwhile, preheat the oven to 200°C/400°F/Gas Mark 6. Brush an ovenproof dish with oil. Cook the potatoes in a pan of salted boiling water for 15–20 minutes, until tender but not falling apart. Drain well and cut into thick slices. Gently toss the slices in the oil and put them around the sides of the prepared dish. Put the fish in the centre.

3. Spoon half the sauce evenly over the fish. Stir the breadcrumbs and cheese into the remainder and spoon it over the fish. Bake in the preheated oven for 15–20 minutes, until the fish flakes easily. Garnish with parsley and serve immediately.

Serves 4

12 new potatoes

1 tbsp olive oil, plus extra for brushing

4 salmon fillets

85 g/3 oz fresh breadcrumbs

55 g/2 oz Parmesan cheese, grated

salt

chopped fresh flat-leaf parsley, to garnish

Tomato sauce

- 25 g/1 oz butter
- 2 tbsp olive oil
- 2 onions, finely chopped
- 2 garlic cloves, finely chopped
- 1 celery stick, finely chopped
- 400 g/14 oz canned chopped tomatoes
- 2 tbsp tomato purée
- brown sugar, to taste
- 1 tbsp chopped fresh marjoram
  100 ml/3½ fl oz dry white wine
- salt and pepper

Fish with Tomato, Garlic & Olive Sauce

1. First, make the sauce. Melt the butter with the oil in a saucepan. Add the onions, garlic, celery and peppers and cook over a low heat, stirring occasionally, for 5 minutes, until softened. Stir in the tomatoes, tomato purée, sugar to taste, olives and water and season to taste with salt and pepper. Increase the heat to medium and bring to the boil, then reduce the heat and simmer, stirring occasionally, for 30 minutes, until thickened.

2. Meanwhile, preheat the oven to 230°C/450°F/Gas Mark 8. Grease a large ovenproof dish, large enough to hold the fish in a single layer, with butter. Mix together the breadcrumbs, parsley and lemon rind in a shallow dish. Beat the egg with the milk in a separate shallow dish. Dip the fish fillets, one at a time, in the egg mixture and then in the breadcrumb mixture and put into the prepared dish. Melt the butter and drizzle a little of it over the fish. Bake in the preheated oven, drizzling frequently with the remaining melted butter, for 15 minutes, until the flesh flakes easily.

3. Remove the fish from the oven and carefully transfer to a warmed serving dish. Spoon the sauce over the top and serve immediately.

Serves 4

115 g/4 oz dry breadcrumbs

2 tbsp finely chopped fresh parsley

finely grated rind of 1 lemon

1 egg

4 tbsp milk

8 plaice or lemon sole fillets

55 g/2 oz butter, plus extra for greasing

Tomato, garlic & olive sauce
* 25 g/1 oz butter
* 2 tbsp olive oil
* 2 onions, thinly sliced
* 2 garlic cloves, very finely chopped
* 1 celery stick, finely chopped
  1 green pepper and 1 red pepper, deseeded and sliced
* 500 g/1 lb 2 oz tomatoes, peeled, cored and sliced
* 2 tbsp tomato purée
* brown sugar, to taste
  12 Kalamata olives, stoned
* 100 ml/3½ fl oz water
* salt and pepper

Monkfish with Tomato, Olive & Caper Sauce

1. First, make the sauce. Melt the butter with the oil in a saucepan. Add the shallots, garlic and celery and cook over a low heat, stirring occasionally, for 5 minutes, until softened. Stir in the tomatoes, sun-dried tomato paste, sugar to taste, capers, olives and Pernod and season to taste with salt and pepper. Increase the heat to medium and bring to the boil, then reduce the heat and simmer, stirring occasionally, for 20–25 minutes, until thickened.

2. Meanwhile, put the fish in a large pan in a single layer. Pour in the wine, add the orange rind, peppercorns and bay leaf and bring just to the boil over a medium heat. Reduce the heat so that the water is barely bubbling, cover and poach for 10–15 minutes, until the flesh flakes easily.

3. Using a fish slice, transfer the fish to a warmed serving dish. Strain the cooking liquid into the sauce and bring to the boil. Boil, stirring constantly, for 2–3 minutes, until reduced. Pour the sauce over the fish and serve immediately.

Serves 4

4 monkfish fillets, about 225 g/8 oz each

150 ml/5 fl oz dry white wine

thinly pared strip of orange rind

6 black peppercorns

1 bay leaf

Tomato, olive & caper sauce

25 g/1 oz butter

2 tbsp olive oil

2 shallots, finely chopped

2 garlic cloves, finely chopped

1 celery stick, finely chopped

500 g/1 lb 2 oz plum tomatoes, peeled, cored and chopped

2 tbsp sun-dried tomato paste

brown sugar, to taste

1 tbsp capers, rinsed

55 g/2 oz black olives, stoned

1 tbsp Pernod

salt and pepper

75

Pissaladière

1. Preheat the oven to 200°C/400°F/Gas Mark 6. Roll out the pastry on a lightly floured surface and use to line a 25-cm/10-inch loose-based tart tin. Prick the base with a fork, line with greaseproof paper and half-fill with baking beans. Put the tin on a baking sheet and bake in the preheated oven for 10 minutes. Remove the paper and beans, return the tin to the oven and bake for a further 10 minutes, until lightly coloured. Remove from the oven and leave to cool.

2. Meanwhile, make the sauce. Melt the butter with the oil in a saucepan. Add the onion, garlic and celery and cook over a low heat, stirring occasionally, for 5 minutes, until softened. Stir in the canned tomatoes, sun-dried tomatoes, tomato purée, sugar to taste and water and season to taste with salt and pepper. Increase the heat to medium and bring to the boil, then reduce the heat and simmer, stirring occasionally, for 15–20 minutes, until thickened.

3. Remove the pan from the heat and stir in the basil. Spread the sauce evenly over the base of the pastry case. Sprinkle with the cheese and arrange the anchovies in a lattice pattern on top. Put an olive half in each diamond shape. Drizzle with oil and, if you want to serve the pissaladière piping hot, return to the oven for 10–15 minutes. Alternatively, serve immediately or leave to cool completely.

Serves 4

250 g/9 oz ready-made shortcrust pastry

plain flour, for dusting

3 tbsp grated Parmesan cheese

50 g/1¾ oz canned anchovy fillets, drained

55 g/2 oz black olives, stoned and halved

olive oil, for drizzling

Tomato sauce

* 25 g/1 oz butter
* 2 tbsp olive oil
* 1 onion, finely chopped
* 2 garlic cloves, finely chopped
* 1 celery stick, finely chopped
* 400 g/14 oz canned chopped tomatoes
* 2 tbsp sliced sun-dried tomatoes in oil
* 2 tbsp tomato purée
* brown sugar, to taste
* 100 ml/3½ fl oz water
* 1 tbsp chopped fresh basil
* salt and pepper

Baked Gnocchi with Tomato Sauce

1. To make the gnocchi, whisk the egg yolks with the granulated sugar in a saucepan until pale and creamy. Sift the flour, cornflour and salt into a bowl, then gradually beat into the egg yolk mixture. Stir in the melted butter and 85 g/3 oz of the Parmesan. Set the pan over a medium heat and gradually stir in the milk. Cook, stirring constantly, for 3–4 minutes, until thick and smooth. Remove the pan from the heat and turn out the mixture onto a baking sheet rinsed with cold water. Spread out to a thickness of 1 cm/½ inch and smooth the surface. Chill in the refrigerator for 30 minutes.

2. Meanwhile, make the sauce. Melt the butter with the oil in a saucepan. Add the onion, garlic and celery and cook over a low heat, stirring occasionally, for 5 minutes, until softened. Stir in the tomatoes, tomato purée, brown sugar to taste, vermouth, parsley and water and season to taste with salt and pepper. Increase the heat to medium and bring to the boil, then reduce the heat and simmer, stirring occasionally, for 25–30 minutes, until thickened.

3. Preheat the oven to 190°C/375°F/Gas Mark 5. Grease an ovenproof dish with butter. Cut the gnocchi into 3–4-cm/1¼–1½-inch squares and put them into the prepared dish, slightly overlapping. Bake in the preheated oven for 15 minutes. Pour the tomato sauce over the top and bake for a further 5–10 minutes, until hot. Sprinkle with the remaining Parmesan, garnish with parsley and serve immediately.

Serves 4

4 egg yolks

2 tsp granulated sugar

55 g/2 oz plain flour

2 tbsp cornflour

pinch of salt

55 g/2 oz butter, melted, plus extra for greasing

115 g/4 oz Parmesan cheese, grated

425 ml/15 fl oz milk

Tomato sauce

* 25 g/1 oz butter
* 2 tbsp olive oil
* 1 onion, finely chopped
* 2 garlic cloves, finely chopped
* 1 celery stick, finely chopped
* 800 g/1 lb 12 oz canned chopped tomatoes
* 2 tbsp tomato purée
* brown sugar, to taste
* 1 tbsp dry vermouth
* 1 tbsp chopped fresh flat-leaf parsley, plus extra to garnish
* 5 tbsp water
* salt and pepper

Cheese-stuffed Onions with Tomato Sauce

1. Preheat the oven to 200°C/400°F/Gas Mark 6. Grease an ovenproof dish, just large enough to hold the onions in a single layer, with butter. Cook the whole peeled onions in a large pan of boiling water for 15 minutes, until tender. Drain and leave to cool, then carefully scoop out the centres without piercing the shells.

2. Finely chop the scooped-out onion and put it into a bowl with the breadcrumbs and cheese. Season to taste with salt and pepper and mix well. Spoon the mixture into the onion shells, packing it down well and doming the tops. Put the onions into the prepared dish, dot with the butter and bake in the preheated oven for 20–30 minutes, until golden brown and tender.

3. Meanwhile, make the sauce. Melt the butter with the oil in a saucepan. Add the spring onions, garlic, celery and carrot and cook over a low heat, stirring occasionally, for 5 minutes, until softened. Stir in the tomatoes, tomato purée, sugar to taste, parsley, chives, wine and Worcestershire sauce and season to taste with salt and pepper. Increase the heat to medium and bring to the boil, then reduce the heat and simmer, stirring occasionally, for 15–20 minutes, until thickened.

4. When the onions are cooked through, transfer them to a warmed serving dish. Spoon the sauce around them and serve immediately.

Serves 4

4 large onions

4 tbsp fresh breadcrumbs

115 g/4 oz Cheddar cheese, grated

25 g/1 oz butter, plus extra for greasing

salt and pepper

Tomato sauce

15 g/½ oz butter

1 tbsp olive oil

2 spring onions, finely chopped

1 garlic clove, finely chopped

1 small celery stick, finely chopped

1 small carrot, finely chopped

200 g/7 oz canned chopped tomatoes

1 tbsp tomato purée

brown sugar, to taste

1 tbsp chopped fresh parsley

1 tbsp snipped fresh chives

50 ml/2 fl oz red wine

1 tbsp Worcestershire sauce

salt and pepper

78

Cauliflower Casserole

1. First, make the sauce. Melt the butter with the oil in a saucepan. Add the onion, garlic and celery and cook over a low heat, stirring occasionally, for 5 minutes, until softened. Stir in the tomatoes, tomato purée, sugar to taste, parsley and water and season to taste with salt and pepper. Increase the heat to medium and bring to the boil, then reduce the heat and simmer, stirring occasionally, for 15–20 minutes, until thickened.

2. Meanwhile, preheat the oven to 190°C/375°F/Gas Mark 5. Grease an ovenproof dish with butter. Bring a large pan of salted water to the boil, add the cauliflower and cook over a medium heat for 10–12 minutes, until tender. Drain well and tip into the prepared casserole.

3. Spoon the tomato sauce over the cauliflower. Mix together the breadcrumbs, Gruyère and Parmesan in a bowl and sprinkle over the top. Drizzle with the melted butter and bake in the preheated oven for 30 minutes, until the topping is golden brown. Serve immediately.

Serves 4

1 large cauliflower,
   cut into florets

2 tbsp fresh white
   breadcrumbs

2 tbsp grated Gruyère cheese

2 tbsp grated Parmesan cheese

55 g/2 oz butter, melted,
   plus extra for greasing

salt

Tomato sauce

* 25 g/1 oz butter
* 2 tbsp olive oil
* 1 onion, finely chopped
* 2 garlic cloves, finely chopped
* 1 celery stick, finely chopped
* 500 g/1 lb 2 oz plum tomatoes,
   peeled, cored and chopped
* 2 tbsp tomato purée
* brown sugar, to taste
* 1–2 tbsp chopped fresh
   flat-leaf parsley
* 100 ml/3½ fl oz water
* salt and pepper

Baked Cheese & Aubergine Layers

1. First, make the sauce. Melt the butter with the oil in a saucepan. Add the shallot, garlic and celery and cook over a low heat, stirring occasionally, for 5 minutes, until softened. Stir in the tomatoes, tomato purée, sugar to taste, oregano and water and season to taste with salt and pepper. Increase the heat to medium and bring to the boil, then reduce the heat and simmer, stirring occasionally, for 15–20 minutes, until thickened.

2. Meanwhile, preheat the oven to 180°C/350°F/Gas Mark 4. Spread out the flour on a shallow dish and season to taste with salt and pepper. Dip the aubergine slices in the flour to coat and shake off any excess. Heat the oil in a frying pan, add the aubergine slices, in batches, and cook for 2 minutes on each side, until lightly browned. Remove and drain on kitchen paper.

3. Make alternating layers of aubergine slices, mozzarella slices and tomato sauce in an ovenproof dish. Sprinkle with the Parmesan and bake in the preheated oven for 25 minutes, until the topping is golden and bubbling. Serve immediately.

Serves 6

55 g/2 oz plain flour

2 large aubergines, sliced

6 tbsp olive oil

225 g/8 oz mozzarella cheese, thinly sliced

55 g/2 oz Parmesan cheese, grated

salt and pepper

Tomato sauce

* 15 g/½ oz butter
* 1 tbsp olive oil
* 1 shallot, finely chopped
* 1 garlic clove, finely chopped
* 1 small celery stick, finely chopped
* 200 g/7 oz canned chopped tomatoes
* 1 tbsp tomato purée
* brown sugar, to taste
* ½ tsp dried oregano
* 50 ml/2 fl oz water
* salt and pepper

Hoppin' John

1. Put the beans into a large saucepan and pour in water to cover. Bring to the boil and boil vigorously for 15 minutes, then remove from the heat and drain. Return the beans to the pan and pour in the 1.2 litres/2 pints of water. Bring to the boil, then reduce the heat, partially cover the pan and simmer for 1½ hours.

2. Meanwhile, make the sauce. Melt the butter with the oil in a saucepan. Add the onion and cook over a low heat, stirring occasionally, for 5 minutes, until softened. Stir in the tomatoes, tomato purée, sugar to taste, cayenne and water and season to taste with salt and pepper. Increase the heat to medium and bring to the boil, then reduce the heat and simmer, stirring occasionally, for 15 minutes, until thickened.

3. Stir the rice into the pan of beans, cover and simmer for a further 15 minutes.

4. Stir the sauce into the bean and rice mixture, re-cover the pan and simmer for a further 15–20 minutes, until the rice and beans are tender. Serve immediately.

Serves 6

225 g/8 oz dried black-eyed beans, soaked overnight and drained

1.2 litres/2 pints water

225 g/8 oz long-grain rice

Tomato sauce
* 25 g/1 oz butter
* 2 tbsp corn oil
* 1 onion, finely chopped
* 400 g/14 oz canned chopped tomatoes
* 2 tbsp tomato purée
* brown sugar, to taste
  ½ tsp cayenne pepper
* 100 ml/3½ fl oz water
* salt and pepper

Special

Steak Pizzaiola

1 First, make the sauce. Melt the butter with the oil in a saucepan. Add the onion and garlic and cook over a low heat, stirring occasionally, for 5 minutes, until softened. Stir in the tomatoes, tomato purée, sugar to taste, olives, basil, oregano and water and season to taste with salt and pepper. Increase the heat to medium and bring to the boil, then reduce the heat and simmer, stirring occasionally, for 15–20 minutes, until thickened.

2 Heat the oil in a large frying pan. Add the steaks and cook over a medium heat for 2–3 minutes on each side. Spoon the sauce over each steak and cook for a further 5 minutes. Serve immediately.

Serves 4

3 tbsp olive oil

4 porterhouse steaks, about 225 g/8 oz each

Pizzaiola sauce

✳ 25 g/1 oz butter

✳ 2 tbsp olive oil

✳ 1 onion, finely chopped

✳ 2 garlic cloves, finely chopped

✳ 500 g/1 lb 2 oz plum tomatoes, peeled, cored and chopped

✳ 2 tbsp tomato purée

✳ brown sugar, to taste

115 g/4 oz green olives, stoned and quartered

✳ 1 tbsp chopped fresh basil

✳ 1 tsp dried oregano

✳ 100 ml/3½ fl oz water

✳ salt and pepper

Stuffed Veal Rolls in Tomato & Wine Sauce

1. Heat the oil in a large flameproof casserole. Add the sausages and cook over a medium heat, turning frequently, for 8–10 minutes, until evenly browned. Transfer to a plate and leave to cool. Pour off the fat from the casserole.

2. To make the sauce, melt the butter with the oil in the casserole. Add the onion, garlic and celery and cook over a low heat, stirring occasionally, for 5 minutes, until softened. Stir in the tomatoes, tomato purée, sugar to taste, marjoram and wine and season to taste with salt and pepper. Increase the heat to medium and bring to the boil, then reduce the heat and simmer, stirring occasionally, for 15–20 minutes, until thickened.

3. Meanwhile, preheat the oven to 180°C/350°F/Gas Mark 4. Lay the escalopes flat on a work surface. Put a sausage on the end of each and roll up, then secure with a wooden cocktail stick. Melt the butter in a frying pan. Add the veal rolls and cook over a medium heat, turning occasionally, for 6–8 minutes, until evenly browned. Remove the pan from the heat and transfer the rolls to the casserole.

4. Cover the casserole, transfer to the preheated oven and bake for 40–45 minutes, until the meat is cooked through and tender. Remove the cocktail sticks from the rolls and serve immediately.

Serves 4

1 tbsp olive oil
4 Italian cooking sausages, such as luganega
4 veal escalopes
55 g/2 oz butter

Tomato & wine sauce
* 25 g/1 oz butter
* 2 tbsp olive oil
* 1 onion, finely chopped
* 2 garlic cloves, finely chopped
* 1 celery stick, finely chopped
* 400 g/14 oz canned chopped tomatoes
* 2 tbsp tomato purée
* brown sugar, to taste
* 1 tbsp chopped fresh marjoram
  300 ml/10 fl oz dry white wine
* salt and pepper

85

Pork Chops in Tomato & Green Pepper Sauce

1. Season the chops well with salt and pepper. Melt the butter with the oil in a large frying pan. Add the chops and cook over a medium heat for 3–4 minutes on each side, until lightly browned. Transfer to a plate and keep warm.

2. Add the onion, garlic, celery and peppers to the pan, reduce the heat and cook, stirring occasionally, for 5 minutes, until softened. Stir in the mushrooms and cook, stirring frequently, for a further 3 minutes. Stir in the tomatoes, tomato purée, sugar to taste, basil, thyme, bay leaf and wine and season to taste with salt and pepper. Increase the heat to medium and bring to the boil. Return the chops to the pan, reduce the heat, cover and simmer, spooning the sauce over the chops frequently, for 40 minutes, until the meat is tender and cooked through.

3. Transfer the chops to a warmed serving dish and keep warm. Mix the cornflour to a paste with the water in a small bowl, then stir into the pan. Cook, stirring constantly, for 3–5 minutes, until thickened. Remove and discard the bay leaf and spoon the sauce over the chops. Garnish with parsley and serve immediately.

Serves 4

4 pork chops
- 25 g/1 oz butter
- 2 tbsp olive oil
- 1 onion, finely chopped
- 2 garlic cloves, finely chopped
- 1 celery stick, finely chopped
  2 green peppers, deseeded and finely chopped
  175 g/6 oz small button mushrooms
- 400 g/14 oz canned chopped tomatoes
- 2 tbsp tomato purée
- brown sugar, to taste
- 1 tbsp chopped fresh basil
- ½ tsp chopped fresh thyme
- 1 bay leaf
  100 ml/3½ fl oz red wine
  1 tbsp cornflour
- 2 tbsp water
- salt and pepper
  chopped fresh flat-leaf parsley, to garnish

86

Lamb with Tomato & Aubergine Sauce

1. First, make the sauce. Melt the butter with the oil in a saucepan. Add the onion, garlic and aubergine and cook over a low heat, stirring occasionally, for 5 minutes, until softened. Stir in the tomatoes, tomato purée, sugar to taste, parsley, bay leaf and water and season to taste with salt and pepper. Increase the heat to medium and bring to the boil, then reduce the heat and simmer, stirring occasionally, for 30 minutes, until thickened.

2. Meanwhile, heat the oil in a frying pan. Add the onions and cook over a low heat, stirring occasionally, for 5 minutes, until softened. Remove with a slotted spoon and drain on kitchen paper, then set aside and keep warm.

3. Return the pan to the heat and melt the butter. Add the lamb noisettes and cook over a medium heat for 4–6 minutes on each side, until tender and cooked to your liking. Transfer to warmed serving plates. Remove and discard the bay leaf from the sauce and divide the sauce among the plates. Top the lamb with the reserved fried onions, garnish with parsley and serve immediately.

Serves 4

1 tbsp olive oil
2 onions, sliced
25 g/1 oz butter
8 lamb noisettes

Tomato & aubergine sauce

* 25 g/1 oz butter
* 2 tbsp olive oil
* 1 onion, sliced
* 2 garlic cloves, finely chopped
* 1 large aubergine, sliced
* 500 g/1 lb 2 oz plum tomatoes, peeled, cored and chopped
* 2 tbsp tomato purée
* brown sugar, to taste
* 1 tbsp chopped fresh parsley, plus extra to garnish
* 1 bay leaf
* 100 ml/3½ fl oz water
* salt and pepper

Lamb Chops in Tomato Sauce with Broad Beans

1. Season the chops with salt and pepper to taste. Melt the butter with the oil in a large frying pan. Add the chops and cook over a medium heat for 1–1½ minutes on each side, until evenly browned. Remove the chops from the pan and set aside.

2. Add the onion, garlic, celery and pancetta to the pan and cook over a low heat, stirring occasionally, for 5 minutes, until the onion has softened. Stir in the tomatoes, tomato purée, sugar to taste, basil, vinegar and water and season to taste with salt and pepper. Increase the heat to medium and bring to the boil, then reduce the heat and simmer, stirring occasionally, for 10 minutes.

3. Return the chops to the pan and add the broad beans. Partially cover and simmer for 10 minutes, until the lamb is tender and cooked through. Transfer to a warmed serving dish and serve immediately.

Serves 4

8 lamb chops
* 25 g/1 oz butter
* 2 tbsp olive oil
* 1 onion, finely chopped
* 2 garlic cloves, finely chopped
* 1 celery stick, finely chopped
40 g/1½ oz pancetta or bacon, diced
* 400 g/14 oz canned chopped tomatoes
* 2 tbsp tomato purée
* brown sugar, to taste
* 2 tbsp chopped fresh basil
1 tbsp red wine vinegar
* 100 ml/3½ fl oz water
350 g/12 oz shelled fresh or frozen broad beans, grey skins removed
* salt and pepper

Spanish Chicken with Tomato & Chocolate Sauce

1. Dust the chicken portions with flour. Heat the oil in a large frying pan. Add the chicken, in batches if necessary, and cook over a medium heat, turning occasionally, for 8–10 minutes, until evenly browned. Remove the chicken from the pan and drain on kitchen paper.

2. Drain off the fat from the pan and wipe out with kitchen paper. To make the sauce, melt the butter with the oil in the same pan. Add the onion, garlic and red pepper and cook over a low heat, stirring occasionally, for 5 minutes, until softened. Stir in the tomatoes, tomato purée, sugar to taste, nutmeg, cinnamon, cloves and wine and season to taste with salt and pepper. Increase the heat to medium and bring to the boil.

3. Return the chicken to the pan, reduce the heat, cover and simmer for 20 minutes. Remove the lid from the pan and simmer for a further 20 minutes, until the chicken is cooked through and tender and the sauce has thickened. Add the chopped chocolate and stir constantly until it has melted. Garnish with grated chocolate and serve immediately.

Serves 6

6 chicken portions
plain flour, for dusting
4 tbsp olive oil

Tomato & chocolate sauce
* 25 g/1 oz butter
* 2 tbsp olive oil
* 1 onion, finely chopped
* 2 garlic cloves, finely chopped
  1 red pepper, deseeded and sliced
* 800 g/1 lb 12 oz canned chopped tomatoes
* 2 tbsp tomato purée
* brown sugar, to taste
  ½ tsp ground nutmeg
  ½ tsp ground cinnamon
  ¼ tsp ground cloves
  250 ml/9 fl oz dry white wine
  70 g/2½ oz dark chocolate, finely chopped, plus extra grated chocolate to garnish
* salt and pepper

89

Chicken in Tomato & Almond Sauce

1. Melt the butter with the oil in a saucepan. Add the shallots, garlic and celery and cook over a low heat, stirring occasionally, for 5 minutes, until softened. Remove the pan from the heat and stir in the ground almonds, breadcrumbs, parsley, tomatoes, tomato purée and sugar to taste. Season to taste with salt and pepper. Return the pan to the heat and cook, stirring constantly, for 5 minutes, or until thickened. Remove the pan from the heat.

2. Put the chicken into a large, shallow pan. Pour in the hot stock and orange juice, add the bouquet garni and peppercorns and bring just to the boil. Reduce the heat so that the water is barely shivering, cover and poach for 20 minutes, until the chicken is cooked through and tender.

3. Transfer the chicken to a warmed serving dish and keep warm. Strain and reserve 5 tablespoons of the cooking liquid, then stir it into the sauce. Return the pan to the heat and cook, stirring constantly, until thoroughly combined and heated through. Pour the sauce over the chicken and sprinkle with the flaked almonds. Garnish with parsley and serve immediately.

Serves 4

* 25 g/1 oz butter
* 2 tbsp olive oil
  2 shallots, finely chopped
* 3 garlic cloves, finely chopped
* 1 celery stick, finely chopped
  55 g/2 oz ground almonds
  4 tbsp fresh breadcrumbs
* 3 tbsp chopped fresh flat-leaf parsley, plus extra to garnish
* 500 g/1 lb 2 oz plum tomatoes, peeled, cored and chopped
* 2 tbsp tomato purée
* brown sugar, to taste
  4 skinless, boneless chicken breasts
  1 litre/1¾ pints hot chicken stock
  juice of ½ orange
  1 bouquet garni
  6 black peppercorns
  2 tbsp flaked almonds
* salt and pepper

Duck with Tomato & Orange Sauce

1. First, make the sauce. Melt the butter with the oil in a saucepan. Add the shallots, garlic and celery and cook over a low heat, stirring occasionally, for 5 minutes, until softened. Stir in the tomatoes, tomato purée, sugar, stock, orange juice, wine and vinegar and season to taste with salt and pepper. Increase the heat to medium and bring to the boil, then reduce the heat and simmer, stirring occasionally, for 20–30 minutes, until thickened.

2. Heat a griddle pan. Score the skin of the duck breasts through to the flesh. When the griddle pan is hot, add the duck breasts, skin-side down, and cook for 8–10 minutes. Turn them over and cook for a further 4–6 minutes on the other side.

3. Meanwhile, remove the pan of sauce from the heat and leave to cool slightly. Ladle it into a food processor or blender and process to a purée. Pass the purée through a sieve into a clean pan and heat through gently. If you prefer a thicker sauce, bring to the boil and boil, stirring constantly, until reduced.

4. Divide the sauce among four warmed individual plates. Top each with a duck breast, garnish with basil leaves and serve immediately.

Serves 4

4 Barbary duck breasts
fresh basil leaves, to garnish

Tomato & orange sauce
- 25 g/1 oz butter
- 2 tbsp olive oil
- 2 shallots, finely chopped
- 1 garlic clove, finely chopped
- 1 celery stick, finely chopped
- 500 g/1 lb 2 oz plum tomatoes, peeled, cored and chopped
- 2 tbsp tomato purée
- 1 tsp brown sugar
- 3 tbsp chicken stock
- juice of 2 oranges
- 2 tbsp dry white wine
- 1 tsp white wine vinegar
- salt and pepper

Halibut in Tomato & Wine Sauce

1. Mix together the flour, coriander, oregano and ½ teaspoon of each salt and pepper in a shallow dish. Coat the fish fillets in the seasoned flour, shaking off the excess. Melt the butter with the oil in a large frying pan. Add the fish and cook over a medium heat for 5 minutes on each side, until evenly browned. Remove with a fish slice and keep warm.

2. Add the shallots, garlic and celery to the pan, reduce the heat to low and cook, stirring occasionally, for 5 minutes, until softened. Stir in the tomatoes, tomato purée, sugar to taste, bay leaf, wine and vinegar and season to taste with salt and pepper. Increase the heat to medium and bring to the boil. Return the fish to the pan and add the prawns. Reduce the heat, cover and simmer for 20 minutes, until the fish flakes easily.

3. Transfer the halibut and prawns to a warmed serving dish and keep warm. Increase the heat to high and bring the sauce to the boil, stirring constantly. Cook, stirring frequently, for 3–4 minutes, until reduced and thickened. Remove and discard the bay leaf and pour the sauce over the fish and prawns. Serve immediately.

Serves 4

- 4 tbsp plain flour
- 1 tbsp finely chopped fresh coriander
- ½ tsp dried oregano
- 4 halibut fillets, about 175 g/6 oz each
- 25 g/1 oz butter
- 2 tbsp olive oil
- 2 shallots, finely chopped
- 1 garlic clove, finely chopped
- 1 celery stick, finely chopped
- 1 kg/2 lb 4 oz plum tomatoes, peeled, deseeded and chopped
- 2 tbsp tomato purée
- brown sugar, to taste
- 1 bay leaf
- 300 ml/10 fl oz dry white wine
- 2 tbsp tarragon vinegar
- 225 g/8 oz raw prawns, peeled and deveined
- salt and pepper

92

Sliced Fish in Chinese Tomato Sauce

1. Cut the fish into 2.5 cm/1 inch wide strips. Mix together the cornflour, ground ginger and salt in a shallow dish, add the fish and toss gently. Gently stir in the egg white.

2. Heat the oil in a large frying pan. Carefully add the pieces of fish, in batches if necessary, and cook over a medium heat, tilting the pan so that the oil flows around them, for 1 minute. Using a fish slice, turn them over and cook for a further 30 seconds. Remove with the fish slice and keep warm. Drain off the oil and wipe out the pan with kitchen paper, then return to the heat.

3. To make the sauce, melt the butter with the oil in the same pan. Add the spring onions, garlic and fresh ginger, reduce the heat and cook, stirring occasionally, for 5 minutes, until softened. Stir in the tomatoes and cook, stirring constantly, for 5 minutes. Stir in the tomato purée, sugar to taste and soy sauce.

4. Mix together the cornflour, stock and rice wine in a bowl until thoroughly combined, then stir into the pan. Increase the heat to medium and cook, stirring constantly, for a few minutes, until thickened. Return the pieces of fish to the pan, reduce the heat to low and simmer for 2–3 minutes, until the fish flakes easily. Transfer the fish and sauce to a warmed serving dish, garnish with spring onions and serve immediately.

Serves 4

700 g/1 lb 9 oz plaice fillets, skinned

2 tbsp cornflour

½ tsp ground ginger

1 tsp salt

1 large egg white, lightly beaten

5 tbsp groundnut oil

Chinese tomato sauce

25 g/1 oz butter

2 tbsp groundnut oil

2 spring onions, finely chopped, plus extra to garnish

2 garlic cloves, finely chopped

2.5-cm/1-inch piece fresh ginger, finely chopped

500 g/1 lb 2 oz plum tomatoes, peeled, cored and chopped

2 tbsp tomato purée

brown sugar, to taste

3 tbsp light soy sauce

2 tsp cornflour

5 tbsp fish stock

2 tbsp Chinese rice wine or dry sherry

Baked Sole with Tomato & Anchovy Sauce

1. First, make the sauce. Melt the butter with the oil in a saucepan. Add the onions and celery and cook over a low heat, stirring occasionally, for 5 minutes, until softened. Stir in the tomatoes, tomato purée, sugar to taste, anchovy essence, marjoram and water and season to taste with salt and pepper. Increase the heat to medium and bring to the boil, then reduce the heat and simmer, stirring occasionally, for 15–20 minutes, until thickened.

2. Meanwhile, preheat the oven to 190°C/375°F/Gas Mark 5. Lightly grease a large ovenproof dish with butter. Put the sole fillets into the dish.

3. Pour the sauce over the fish and bake in the preheated oven for 30 minutes, until the flesh flakes easily. Sprinkle with the chives and gherkins and serve immediately.

Serves 4

butter, for greasing
900 g/2 lb sole fillets
1 tbsp snipped fresh chives
3 pickled gherkins, sliced

Tomato & anchovy sauce
* 25 g/1 oz butter
* 2 tbsp olive oil
* 2 onions, thinly sliced
* 1 celery stick, finely chopped
* 400 g/14 oz canned chopped tomatoes
* 2 tbsp tomato purée
* brown sugar, to taste
  1 tsp anchovy essence
* ½ tsp dried marjoram
* 100 ml/3½ fl oz water
* salt and pepper

Provençal Prawns

1. Melt 25 g/1 oz of the butter with the oil in a large flameproof casserole. Add the prawns and cook, turning frequently, for 3–4 minutes, until they have turned pink. Remove with a slotted spoon and set aside.

2. Add the onion, garlic, celery and peppers to the casserole and cook over a low heat, stirring occasionally, for 5 minutes, until softened. Add the mushrooms and cook, stirring frequently, for a further 2 minutes.

3. Stir in the tomatoes, tomato purée, sugar to taste, thyme, oregano, bay leaf and wine and season to taste with salt and pepper. Increase the heat to medium and bring to the boil, then reduce the heat, cover and simmer, stirring occasionally, for 15 minutes.

4. Meanwhile, put the remaining butter and the flour on a saucer and work together with your fingertips until a smooth paste (beurre manié) forms. Shape into several small balls. Add the beurre manié to the sauce, one piece at a time, stirring constantly. Make sure each piece has been fully incorporated before adding the next. Cook, stirring constantly, for 2–3 minutes. Return the prawns to the casserole and simmer, stirring occasionally, for 5 minutes. Remove and discard the bay leaf. Garnish with thyme and serve immediately.

Serves 6

* 40 g/1½ oz butter
* 2 tbsp olive oil
* 1 kg/2 lb 4 oz raw Mediterranean prawns, peeled and deveined
* 1 small onion, finely chopped
* 3 garlic cloves, finely chopped
* 1 celery stick, finely chopped
* 1 red pepper and 1 yellow pepper, deseeded and chopped
* 225 g/8 oz button mushrooms, halved
* 500 g/1 lb 2 oz plum tomatoes, peeled, cored and chopped
* 2 tbsp tomato purée
* brown sugar, to taste
* 1 tbsp chopped fresh thyme, plus extra to garnish
* ½ tsp dried oregano
* 1 bay leaf
* 150 ml/5 fl oz dry white wine
* 2 tbsp plain flour
* salt and pepper

95

Mussels Baked in Tomato & Basil Sauce

1. Scrub the mussels under cold running water and pull off the beards. Discard any with broken shells and any that refuse to close when tapped. Put the lemon slices in a heavy saucepan, add the mussels and pour in the wine. Cover and cook over a high heat, shaking the pan occasionally, for 4–6 minutes, until the shells have opened. Remove with a slotted spoon and discard any mussels that remain closed. Strain the cooking liquid through a muslin-lined strainer into a bowl.

2. To make the sauce, melt the butter with the oil in a saucepan. Add the shallots, garlic and celery and cook over a low heat, stirring occasionally, for 5 minutes, until softened. Stir in the tomatoes, tomato purée, sugar to taste, basil, bay leaf and the reserved cooking liquid and season to taste with salt and pepper. Increase the heat to medium and bring to the boil, then reduce the heat and simmer, stirring occasionally, for 15 minutes.

3. Meanwhile, preheat the oven to 180°C/350°F/Gas Mark 4. Grease an ovenproof dish with butter. Remove the mussels from their shells. Mix together the breadcrumbs and cheese.

4. Remove and discard the bay leaf from the sauce and gently stir in the mussels. Pour the mixture into the prepared dish, sprinkle with the breadcrumb mixture and bake in the preheated oven for 20 minutes, until the topping is golden and bubbling. Serve immediately.

Serves 4

2 kg/4 lb 8 oz live mussels

1 lemon, sliced

150 ml/5 fl oz dry white wine

butter, for greasing

2 tbsp fresh breadcrumbs

55 g/2 oz Parmesan cheese, grated

Tomato & basil sauce

25 g/1 oz butter

2 tbsp olive oil

4 shallots, finely chopped

3 garlic cloves, finely chopped

2 celery sticks, finely chopped

600 g/1 lb 5 oz canned chopped tomatoes

2 tbsp tomato purée

brown sugar, to taste

3 tbsp chopped fresh basil

1 bay leaf

salt and pepper

Scallops in Tomato Sauce

1. First, make the sauce. Melt the butter with the oil in a saucepan. Add the shallots and whole garlic clove and cook over a low heat, stirring occasionally, for 5 minutes, until softened. Stir in the tomatoes, tomato purée, sugar to taste, dill, parsley, mint and water and season to taste with salt and pepper. Increase the heat to medium and bring to the boil, then reduce the heat and simmer, stirring occasionally, for 15–20 minutes, until thickened.

2. Heat the oil with the sea salt in a non-stick or heavy-based frying pan. Add the scallops and cook for 2 minutes on each side, until golden. Remove from the pan and transfer to a serving dish.

3. Remove and discard the garlic from the sauce and spoon the sauce over the scallops. Garnish with dill and serve immediately.

Serves 4–6

2 tbsp olive oil

1 tbsp coarse sea salt

24 scallops, shelled

Tomato sauce

* 25 g/1 oz butter
* 2 tbsp olive oil
  2 shallots, finely chopped
* 1 garlic clove, peeled
* 500 g/1 lb 2 oz plum tomatoes, peeled, cored and chopped
* 2 tbsp tomato purée
* brown sugar, to taste
* 2 tbsp chopped fresh dill, plus extra to garnish
* 2 tbsp chopped fresh parsley
* 1 tbsp chopped fresh mint
* 100 ml/3½ fl oz water
* salt and pepper

Portuguese Eggs in Tomato Shells

1. Cut a round out of the stalk end of each tomato to make an opening large enough for an egg. Using a teaspoon, carefully scoop out the seeds and pulp, without piercing the shells, and reserve. Season the insides with salt and pepper to taste. Chop the cut-out rounds.

2. Melt the butter with the oil in a saucepan. Add the onion, garlic and celery and cook over a low heat, stirring occasionally, for 5 minutes, until softened. Stir in the reserved tomato seeds, pulp and chopped rounds, the tomato purée, sugar to taste, basil and water and season to taste with salt and pepper. Increase the heat to medium and bring to the boil, then reduce the heat and simmer, stirring occasionally, for 15–20 minutes, until thickened. Remove from the heat and leave to cool.

3. Stand the tomato shells on a serving dish. Shell the eggs and put one egg into each tomato shell. Chill in the refrigerator for at least 30 minutes. Stir the mayonnaise into the cooled tomato sauce, then transfer to a bowl, cover with clingfilm and chill in the refrigerator. To serve, spoon the sauce over the eggs and garnish with watercress and rocket.

Serves 6

6 large tomatoes, peeled
* 25 g/1 oz butter
* 2 tbsp olive oil
* 1 small onion, finely chopped
* 1 garlic clove, finely chopped
* 1 celery stick, finely chopped
* 1 tbsp tomato purée
* brown sugar, to taste
* 1 tbsp chopped fresh basil
* 4 tbsp water
6 hard-boiled eggs
4 tbsp mayonnaise
* salt and pepper
watercress and rocket leaves, to garnish

98

Slow-cooked Potato Stew

1. Parboil the potatoes in a saucepan of salted boiling water for 5 minutes. Drain and set aside.

2. Melt the butter with the oil in a saucepan. Add the pancetta, onion, garlic and celery and cook over a low heat, stirring occasionally, for 5 minutes, until softened. Stir in the tomatoes, tomato purée, sugar to taste, marjoram and stock and season to taste with salt and pepper. Increase the heat to medium and bring to the boil. Gently stir in the potatoes, reduce the heat to very low, cover and simmer, stirring occasionally, for 45–50 minutes, until the potatoes are tender and the sauce has thickened. (Use a fork to stir gently to avoid breaking up the potatoes.)

3. Taste and adjust the seasoning, adding salt and pepper if needed. Transfer the mixture to a warmed serving dish and serve immediately.

Serves 4

700 g/1 lb 9 oz waxy potatoes, cut into 2.5-cm/1-inch cubes

25 g/1 oz butter

2 tbsp olive oil

55 g/2 oz pancetta or bacon, diced

1 onion, finely chopped

1 garlic clove, finely chopped

1 celery stick, finely chopped

400 g/14 oz canned chopped tomatoes

2 tbsp tomato purée

brown sugar, to taste

1 tbsp chopped fresh marjoram

100 ml/3½ fl oz vegetable stock

salt and pepper

Polenta, Cheese & Tomato Sauce Gratin

1. Line a 28 x 18-cm/11 x 7-inch cake tin with clingfilm. Pour the 1 litre/1¾ pints of water into a large saucepan and bring to the boil. Stir the salt into the water. While stirring constantly, pour the polenta into the pan in a steady stream, then cook, stirring constantly, for 5 minutes. Stir in the mace and paprika, then pour the mixture into the prepared tin. Smooth the surface and leave to cool.

2. To make the sauce, melt the butter with the oil in a saucepan. Add the onion, garlic and celery and cook over a low heat, stirring occasionally, for 5 minutes, until softened. Stir in the tomatoes, tomato purée, sugar to taste, parsley and water and season to taste with salt and pepper. Increase the heat to medium and bring to the boil, then reduce the heat and simmer, stirring occasionally, for 15–20 minutes, until thickened.

3. Meanwhile, preheat the oven to 200°C/400°F/Gas Mark 6. Grease an ovenproof dish with butter.

4. Turn out the polenta onto a chopping board and cut into 2.5-cm/1-inch squares. Remove the sauce from the heat. Put half the polenta squares into the prepared dish and spoon half the sauce over them, then sprinkle with half the cheese. Repeat the layers. Bake in the preheated oven for 30 minutes, until the topping is golden brown and bubbling. Serve immediately.

Serves 4

1 litre/1¾ pints water

1 tsp salt

250 g/9 oz quick-cook polenta

pinch of ground mace

1 tsp paprika

butter, for greasing

85 g/3 oz Gruyère or Emmenthal cheese, grated

Tomato sauce

* 25 g/1 oz butter
* 2 tbsp olive oil
* 1 Spanish onion, finely chopped
* 2 garlic cloves, finely chopped
* 1 celery stick, finely chopped
* 800 g/1 lb 12 oz canned chopped tomatoes
* 2 tbsp tomato purée
* brown sugar, to taste
* 1 tbsp chopped fresh flat-leaf parsley
* 100 ml/3½ fl oz water
* salt and pepper

Aubergine & Potato Bake with Tomato Sauce

1. Heat 2 tablespoons of the oil in a large frying pan. Add one third of the aubergines and cook over a medium heat, turning occasionally, for 8–10 minutes, until evenly golden brown. Remove with a slotted spoon and drain on kitchen paper. Cook the remaining aubergine slices in the same way, using 4 tablespoons of the remaining oil.

2. Add the remaining oil to the frying pan and heat. Add the potato slices and cook over a medium heat, turning frequently, for 10 minutes, until evenly golden brown. Remove from the pan.

3. Preheat the oven to 180°C/350°F/Gas Mark 4. Grease an ovenproof dish with butter. Mix together the thyme, pepper and salt in a saucer. Make alternating layers of aubergine and potato slices in the prepared dish and sprinkle with the thyme mixture. Beat together the cream, eggs and nutmeg in a bowl until thoroughly combined, then pour the mixture into the dish. Bake in the preheated oven for 45 minutes, until set.

4. Meanwhile, pour the tomato sauce into a large saucepan and place over a low heat. Heat gently until warmed through.

5. Remove the sauce from the heat and strain into a jug. Remove the dish from the oven, pour the sauce over it and sprinkle with the chives. Serve immediately.

Serves 4

125 ml/4 fl oz olive oil

3 small aubergines, thinly sliced

550 g/1 lb 4 oz potatoes, thinly sliced

butter, for greasing

½ tsp dried thyme

½ tsp pepper

¾ tsp salt

300 ml/10 fl oz single cream

5 eggs

pinch of grated nutmeg

1 quantity Basic Tomato Sauce (see page 10)

2 tbsp snipped fresh chives